More Praise for *American Bastard*

American Bastard has it all: dazzling craft, a resonant story, and an unflinching honesty, the essential ingredient transforming a work into a work of art. This deep dive into the emotional world of an adoptee and her struggle to find the missing and unresolved parts of herself left behind on the day of her adoption is at once disturbing and hypnotic. *American Bastard* is a balancing act, a hybrid work blending prose and poetry that threatens to unravel on the page as the author searches for her history, her identity, and her place in the world.

—**Nikki Moustaki**, author of *Extremely Lightweight Guns*

American Bastard dares and succeeds at reimaging and redefining memoir as a genre where stream of consciousness meets essay, meets magical realism, meets reportage, meets poetry to create an epic mosaic only possible through the literary genius of Jan Beatty. And as if that weren't enough, an enthralling yet gracious exposé about adoption that confronts and educates us through a voice that is at times tender and broken, at times angry and fierce, but always unflinchingly honest with herself, the people in her life, and her readers.

—**Richard Blanco**, author of *The Prince of Los Cocuyos: A Miami Memoir*

T0125895

AMERICAN BASTARD

a memoir

JAN BEATTY

2019
Red Hen Press
Nonfiction
Award

 Red Hen Press | *Pasadena, CA*

Book layout by Mark E. Cull

Library of Congress Cataloging-in-Publication Data

Names: Beatty, Jan, 1952– author.
Title: American bastard : a memoir : Jan Beatty.
Description: First edition. | Pasadena, CA : Red Hen Press, 2021.
Identifiers: LCCN 2021015905 (print) | LCCN 2021015906 (ebook) | ISBN
    9781597098786 (trade paperback) | ISBN 9781636280127 (epub)
Subjects: LCSH: Beatty, Jan, 1952– | Authors, American—20th
    century—Biography. | Adoptees—United States—Biography.
Classification: LCC PS3552.E179 Z46 2021 (print) | LCC PS3552.E179
    (ebook) | DDC 813/.54 [B]—dc23
LC record available at https://lccn.loc.gov/2021015905
LC ebook record available at https://lccn.loc.gov/2021015906

The National Endowment for the Arts, the Los Angeles County Arts Commission, the Ahmanson Foundation, the Dwight Stuart Youth Fund, the Max Factor Family Foundation, the Pasadena Tournament of Roses Foundation, the Pasadena Arts & Culture Commission and the City of Pasadena Cultural Affairs Division, the City of Los Angeles Department of Cultural Affairs, the Audrey & Sydney Irmas Charitable Foundation, the Meta & George Rosenberg Foundation, the Albert and Elaine Borchard Foundation, the Adams Family Foundation, Amazon Literary Partnership, the Sam Francis Foundation, and the Mara W. Breech Foundation partially support Red Hen Press.

First Edition
Published by Red Hen Press
www.redhen.org

Acknowledgments

The author wishes to acknowledge the following journals in which excerpts first appeared, sometimes in different forms:

Black Tongue Review, Creative Nonfiction, HeArt, Paterson Literary Review, Poetry, Rattle, and *San Diego Poetry Annual.*

Other excerpts have appeared in different forms in the following books and anthology:

Boneshaker, Jackknife: New and Selected Poems, Mad River, Red Sugar, The Body Wars, The Switching/Yard, all published by the University of Pittsburgh Press; *Home Ground: A Guide to the American Landscape* (Lopez and Gwartney 2013); *Journey of the Adopted Self* (Lifton 1995); *Maple Leafs Top 100: Toronto's Greatest Players of All Time* (Leonetti and Iaboni 2007); *Show Us Your Papers* (Paff, Buccilli, and Pollard 2020); and *Still Here* (O'Brien 2021).

I would like to express my appreciation to the Pittsburgh Foundation for a grant that helped to fund this book; Brush Creek Residency, where most of this book was put to paper; and the Howard Heinz Endowments; the Pittsburgh Cultural Trust; the Creative Capital Foundation; Paterson Poetry Center; and Leighton Artists' Studios, Banff, Alberta, Canada, for fellowships and support. Thanks to the Carlow University English Department for ongoing support. Special thanks to the wonderful staff at Red Hen Press.

I'd like to thank my family of strangers, teachers, and friends who have helped me over the years as this book was forming. Specifically, the people who helped in the living and writing of the book: Lisa Alexander, Joseph Bathanti, Joan Bauer, Paul Baumgartner, Ann Begler, Patty Bernarding, Gerry Rosella Boccella, Bounce, Mad Dog Brooks, Anita Byerly, Gerry Cassie, Joy Castro, Allison Adelle Hedge Coke, Wanda Coleman, Kay Comini, Jimmy Cvetic, Jennifer Kwon Dobbs, Heather Donohue, Sharon Doubiago, Denise Duhamel, Martin Farawell, Anahita Firouz, Jay Flory, Roberta Foizey, Dr. G., Diane Glancy, Sinead Gleeson, Matt Gordley, Laurie

Graham, Dan Green, David Groff, Michael Jones, James Allen Hall, William Harry Harding, Sharon Hawkins for lifesaving, Katie Hogan, Dorothy Holley, Nancy Koerbel, Gretel Ehrlich, Meg Kearney, Colleen Keegan, Beth Kukucka, Gerry LaFemina, Gail Langstroth, Betty Jean Lifton, Barry Lopez, Peter Oresick, Marilyn Marsh Noll, Maria Mazziotti Gillan, Patty McCollum, Bob McGrogan, Leslie McIlroy, Emily Mohn-Slate, Liane Ellison Norman, Marianne Novy, Jean O'Brien, Sharon Olds, Alicia Ostriker, Wendy Scott Paff, Elicia Parkinson, Bob Patak, D. A. Powell, Deb Pursifull, Anne Rashid, Dr. Robin, Lee Ann Roripaugh, Don Rosenzweig, Joanne Samraney, Kayla Sargeson, Patricia Smith, Tracy K. Smith, Shirley Snodey, Rhoda Mills Sommer, Kathy Staresinic, Jerry Stern, Michele Stoner, Michael Thomas, Brian Turner, Beatrice Vasser, Stacey Waite, Lucienne Wald, Michael Waters, Afaa Michael Weaver, Bruce Weigl, Jill West, Martha West, Sarah Williams-Devereux and all the Madwomen, and Michael Wurster. To the cab driver in Prince Rupert, British Columbia; to Ed, the security guard at the MTS Centre in Winnipeg, home of the Manitoba Hockey Hall of Fame; to VIA Rail for getting me there.

Special thanks to Todd Sanders for generous assistance with photography and cooler-than-Jeff-Goldblum brilliance.

With deep thanks to Richard Blanco, Sandra Cisneros, and Sapphire for your all-out support; to Nikki Moustaki for choosing the book; and especially to my teachers: Maggie Anderson, Patricia Dobler, Lynn Emanuel. Extra thanks to Tamara DiPalma for cover mojo and for being Jack. Big thanks to Nancy Kirkwood, bloodsister of choice; Most of all to my poetry companion and cosmic mentor, Judith Vollmer, for your brave writing and living; my earth teacher, Ed Ochester, for years of help and your killer poems. To Charlotte Thoma, spirit guide; my father of fathers, Robert T. Beatty.

To Don, my true north, my family.

This is for the lost ones who never knew
where they came from

This is against the ones who pretended
the loss never happened

This story begins at an impasse,
since I am writing to you as someone who was
never born.

—Patrice Staiger

[S]he is a fake child. No doubt [s]he was born of a woman, but this origin has not been noted by the social memory. As far as everyone and, consequently, [s]he [her]self are concerned, [s]he appeared one fine day without having been carried in any known womb: [s]he is a synthetic product.

—Jean-Paul Sartre

The tree was shaken from the inside out—

> The tree was shaken from the inside out—
> the party greenly winding the interior stair—
> then abruptly stilled, as if drunkenness,
> resting there, summoned the suddenly
> weighted doubt . . .
> —Lynne McMahon

Let's talk about the tree, the shaking. After the shaking is done, after the child finds out she is not of this family, that there is no one she looks like, shares blood with; that her name is not her name, her family is a lie, her entire life is a lie—there is no more tree.

Maybe you are saying, "I've felt that way—I always thought I was adopted." Please, let me stop you. You weren't.

Talking about the mothered/motherless self, Betty Jean Lifton says: "Those who know their mothers cannot imagine what it is like not to know the woman who brought you into the world. What it is like to be forbidden by law to see her face, hear her voice, know her name. No one can imagine it because it is unimaginable."

Maybe you're saying, "I had the same thing. My mother died when I was ten." Please, let me stop you. I'm sorry for your loss, but this is not that. As tough as that was, you know who you are, you have a family, a face, a bloodline, a medical history.

Maybe you're saying, "At least your family wanted you." Please, let me stop you. Maybe you missed the part when I said the adoptee's family is a lie, her name is a lie, she has no grounding in the world? And besides, this "chosen baby" crap is the biggest lie to ever come down the pike.

This is not about measuring sorrow. But this one's about you— how you can't seem to imagine, not even for a second, how it might be for someone who doesn't know who they are— without boomeranging back to your own life. Try it. Try staying with the foreign idea that a baby is born, then sold to another person. Stay with it. There is the physical trauma of the broken bond. There is the erasure of the baby's entire history. There are these hands that have a different smell, a different DNA—reaching for the baby, calling it theirs. Stay with that for a while. No talking.

When I was young, I was a comet with an unending shimmering tail, and I flew over the brokenness below that was my life. I didn't know until I was twelve that we carry other bodies inside us. Not babies, but bodies of blood that speak to us in plutonic languages of pith and serum.

—*Red Sugar*

one

red dress

i stole it back cuz it was mine from da get-go . . .

all shook up
a rumble mama burped and there i was. take
these rhythms as evidence, my splendid rock-and-roll
                    —Wanda Coleman

After the tearing and rolling

*After the tearing and rolling, you are an infant somewhere. In a crib, in a roomful of cribs? Someone is taking care of you. You don't know who. Who is the person who picks you up? Is it a woman? Is it a nun? There is no story in sight, no same loving face, blood-of-my-blood face. The smells, the feel of the rolling and tearing are gone—gone where? No face who has your face. No way of knowing who is who, what hands are these? Why are they different every time? There is no bonding taking place. The story is fractured here and forever after. Then strangers come to gaze at you, touch you, wonder about you. They decide to pluck you out of there and **make you theirs**. These strangers will take your name away and hide it. The government will cooperate. It will take months and months for this baby trade to be completed—a baby in exchange for money. Meanwhile, someone is feeding you. Is it a kind person? What do they smell like? (You will never know these hands again) You will be taken to a strange place.*

People will start calling you the lucky one, the chosen baby, no one sees that your story is gone, that you are being handed off like a football. From now on, everyone will pretend that your first story never existed, they will act and want you to act as if you are one of them—their blood, their faces, their world. You know that to survive, you will have to do this, you will have to pass. But your new "mother" has dark hair and brown eyes, your "father" has dark hair—their noses are not like yours, your white blonde hair shines sickly like the odd light in a bad painting. Later, you look at your cousins, they have beautiful long eyelashes—all of them—the same. You value how others resemble others—

—you long for it. In first grade you refuse to make a family tree. Your "parents" and teacher suggest you make one based on your new family. You refuse.

They deny the story

They deny the story.

The name on my preamended birth certificate is Patrice Staiger. As far as I know, I was born in Roselia Asylum and Maternity Hospital in 1952, a home for unwed mothers in the Hill District of Pittsburgh, which was run by the Sisters of Charity. As far as I know, which is not nearly far enough. There are ghosts all over the story of my beginnings. No one can be pinned down. Roselia doesn't exist anymore and the records are sealed. A birth certificate takes years to get. The names on the birth certificate don't want to be found. The story itself becomes a ghost.

An entrenched stream or river is one on a flat plain

> An entrenched stream or river is one on a flat
> plain that has cut a trench deep enough to
> contain its flow, even in flood conditions. A
> stream becomes entrenched when some change
> takes it out of equilibrium—a change in climate
> or land use, for example, or the uplift of land
> over which the river flows.
>
> —Michael Collier

Who were these people on my birth certificate? Many adoptees do not search for their birth parents because of the raging fear, guilt, the skill at dissociation that they've developed to even live in the world. Did they want to hear from me? Could I handle whoever they were? I didn't want a family—*I only wanted the story.* Who was I, how did I get here, why did they give me away? It felt like a massive wall of water coming at me, something so large that I couldn't imagine it.

Once I had the names and the numbers on the preamended birth certificate, I found out that my adoption was handled through Catholic Social Services. I called to make an appointment with them, to see if they would give me information on my birthmother. I showed up at the Investment Building on Fourth Avenue in downtown Pittsburgh for my appointment. The blood running through my body—whose was it? Literally shaking and filled with dread, I walked into the meeting.

Raging water followed, the wall of it broke—a woman with a file folder sat five feet from me with all my information before her. She asked me what I wanted, why now? She said that she could contact my birthmother to see if she would meet with me, but that I was unstable. There's nothing we can do for you now. Come back in six months.

After years of not knowing who I am—I'm five feet from the answers to my blood and a woman stonewalls me. I knew if I objected or showed anger, I would be smack in the middle of a catch-22, the power of the state, proving my "instability."

The letter, the crucifix

The letter, the crucifix. I got a call from Catholic Social Services—my birthmother didn't want to see me. She had written a letter that I could come and pick up.

The letter was written on horrible yellow stationery with some sweet blue flowers on the border. When I opened it, a gold crucifix on a chain fell out. *You've got to be kidding me*, I thought. *This* is her idea of a response?

As I read the letter, I was shaking with the excitement of at last having some contact/and with the anger of her not meeting me.

She's talking about her parish priest, and the advice he gave her to give up her child for adoption. How "he" thought it was best.

Her priest? Really? How does a guy who's never given birth . . . ? What business is it of his?

As I'm reading, I'm writing a letter in my head:

> *Dear birthmother:*
>   *Why are you listening to him? Why won't you own it, say what you want, say what you feel? The crucifix was a cheap shot. Think about it. You're sending me a "thing."*

> *An image of a dead guy on a cross—another man.*
> *What is it that you want?*
> *Where's your courage? I deserve more.*

I put the crucifix back in the envelope. I needed a real body, not a dead one.

I wear the red dress

I wear the red dress. I drive downtown for the meeting but am too afraid to go in. After two years, my birthmother has decided to meet with me—after seeing an Oprah show on adoption. Why does Oprah wield more power than a flesh-and-blood daughter? I call my friend Paul, who works at the Welfare office in the State Office building, and he meets me at a bar in Market Square. It's morning, but we drink two shots of cheap whiskey each, and he walks me over to the Investment Building to meet my birthmother.

I'm an alcoholic in recovery for approximately twenty-seven years now. It seems crazy that I would go into that meeting after drinking, but at the same time, it seems that of course I would have a drink first. That was what I did.

I meet the social worker, who leads me to this closed room. She says, "You have forty minutes." I walk in and my birthmother has on a blue cotton V-neck dress. It may seem strange to focus on this. At the time, I worked as a waitress, didn't have much money. I owned two dresses—a red one and a blue one. I decide to wear the red one to this meeting, and my birthmother is wearing the blue one. This is not about the merely instinctual. This is a book about what happened.

It's not as though it's a common dress—a dark blue cotton jersey with a V-neck and a thin tan string-belt. There it is, on her body, the body that I used to live in, apparently. Apparently, because all of this is shocking, more than strange, it's mind-bending, like the ground is sky and the sky is ground. I don't know how to describe it.

I walk in, she jumps up and hugs me, and the hug is the real and unreal mixing somehow—it feels good, but I want to run, I want to get her off of me, because—*who is she? And where has she been?*

We sit on basic chairs a few feet apart in this square room in this office building, and start to try to speak about our lives. She is sobbing hysterically. Deep, ongoing sobs, and saying, "I'm sorry, I'm sorry." It's a shocking and disturbing sight, this woman who I've never seen (except at birth), sitting before me crying and crying.

She has short, dyed blonde hair, light blue eyes. While she sobs, I am studying her to see if this is someone, finally—someone who I might look like. The resemblance is there. It's not overwhelming, but her coloring, her fair skin and bone structure seem to have some similarity to mine. Well, actually, mine to hers.

You might think it cold and strange that I'm studying her in detail while she's crying—this woman who supposedly is my mother. *But the body and blood is everything.* Not knowing if there is another person out there who has your blood, who looks like you. That's everything to an adopted child. I was thirty-two years old when I met my birthmother. But at this first meeting, and still today, I'm the adopted child with a couple pieces of information.

You might imagine, you might want to make it a magical, beautiful meeting between mother and daughter—if so, you would be projecting some cultural story onto this event. I didn't know this woman who I longed to meet and find. I had some questions.

I had assembled huge walls of protection over the years as a way to stay alive. An adoptee needs to have a strategy from a young age, whether conscious or not—a way to manage this hole of abandonment, loss, and grief. It's too much for a child to handle. The loss of identity, the complete erasure of history, the floating in the world without a name. The original loss of being taken from the mother at birth, and then the adoptive parents pretending that they are your parents. The primary, lifelong trauma.

So here I am, sitting across from her. The real and unreal colliding. Holes in the air where something alive, something real might come through. Forty minutes. I feel bad for her, but I want her to stop crying. I think: *this might be the only time I see her. I need to know where I came from. I want the story: how did I get here, how did it happen? Why did she give me away, and the big question, who is my father? I want answers.*

I tell her that I have the same dress at home. "You're kidding," she says. No, I'm not, and I ask her where she bought her shoes. "Bakers," she says. I tell her that I have those same shoes at home. Brown low heels with a strap. Nice shoes. What is that? Does the same blood give us the same fashion sense? It's too strange to take in, and still is. Like a genetic code leading you into a dress store?

She starts to talk, and the questions she has are disturbing to me.

"Did you have a good life?"

I think: *Of course I didn't, you gave me away. What are you talking about, I'm just starting my life, what is a good life, anyway? I'm suicidal, I struggle to stay alive, would you call that good?*

I say, "I guess, I mean it's hard to say."

She says, "Did you do well in school?"

What is she talking about? Why are we talking about this? I don't care how I did in school, and I'm thirty-two years old, who cares about this. Obviously, she does.

I say, "Yeah, I got a degree in Social Work. I'm a waitress now, though."

She says, "Oh, that's wonderful."

I'm thinking: *What's wonderful about it, we're here in this jacked-up room and you're my fucking mother, and you're not going to get down to it? I don't want to talk about this shit with you.*

"Do you have a boyfriend?" she says.

That's it. I'm the shell-shocked adoptee and want to like her and her to like me, but that's it.

"Yes, I have a boyfriend, but what does that have to do with anything?" I say.

She draws back, still crying. She says, "I just want to know that you have a good life."

"I know," I say, "but I need to know what happened."

"What happened?" she says.

"Where I came from, who my father is," I say.

She starts sobbing uncontrollably and grabs my arm, hard.

"You have to promise me that you won't look for him," she says, "he's not a nice man."

More holes in the air. How to get to something alive, something real?

This woman, my mother who I've never met, grabbing me, asking me to promise something so large. It's too much. She hasn't given me any information.

She kept hold of my arm, her voice getting louder: "You have to promise me you won't look for him."

"I promise," I say.

I know that I'm lying. I want her to stop. I don't want to lie, but I want her to stop. This is supposed to be about real. This is supposed to be about truth. The time is running down. I say to myself: *I'll look for him, and I'll find him.*

"Thank you," she says.

She keeps crying, but starts talking.

"You have to understand, it was a different time. I'm so ashamed."

I say, "There's no reason to be ashamed."

She says, "Being pregnant and unmarried was a terrible thing. It brought shame to the family. I had to hide for my whole pregnancy until it was time to have you."

She's sobbing again, "It was terrible. I didn't have any money, I knew I couldn't give you any kind of life. I'm sorry."

I feel bad that she had to go through that. I feel angry that the stupid culture oppressed women like this, and still does— but we are so far away from anything I need to know. She's rubbing her hands together, rubbing her hands over her forearms. I'm looking at her tan, her solid legs, hoping I'll look strong like her when I'm older.

I say, "I don't think there's anything wrong with having sex or getting pregnant. I'm not upset about that. I don't have any moral judgments about it—really. Can you just tell me how things happened, about my father—I won't look for him, but can you tell me how you met him?"

It all starts up again, she sobs harder, louder. She's shaking her head.

"He's not someone you want to know," she says.

And then, "You can't go look for him. You can't."

It is one crazy scene—the room so full of wild emotion, it feels full with pressure. Then I look up at this crying woman and try to understand that she is my mother. It's hard to even believe in the present moment. The "real" seems "unreal." I had been searching for years and hoping and believing in this moment and now finding the body seems like an out-of-body experience. Like we are saying sentences that fly past each other, like we are at such cross-purposes, blood-to-blood, dressed in each other's clothes.

I'm grateful in the swirling of that day. To see her, to have a face, a body that is actual and real. That part is probably the most important. As an adoptee, I need that face, that blood connection to not feel as alone in the world. That is everything. Everything. The meeting is what it is. Who knows what it should be?

We would meet two more times over the years, with very different results. We hug again at the end of the forty minutes.

Forty minutes for a life. Shortly after, I stop wearing dresses, cut my hair shorter and shorter. Dye it blue.

My mother was a dress

For years I was wearing her, she was cotton, her neck a blue V for her blue vagina that birthed six babies. She had a vanilla string around her waist even though she was hooker-red at heart, like me.

I wore her for two years, along with a sister dress of deep cherry. When I went to meet her the first time at Catholic Social Services, I wore the cherry and she wore the blue vagina.

We thought that genetics had made us go to Joseph P. Hornes to buy the V, but decided we both lived near the bloodless department store. After that, I took her off, stopped wearing her, didn't want her touching my body anymore.

I prefer to think it's all animal—the way the V opens my neck to predators, the way she scissored her legs open to my father's cock. The way the dress hugs my hips then falls, just like she said she hugged me once—before falling away, switching me out for sale.

two

treacherous body

The delicate, unfixed condition of love, the
treacherous body.

—D. A. Powell

I can hear the terrible lapping

I can hear the terrible lapping of the water against the docks, the small rocks. My father and I are walking by the lake. I am eight years old and everything is covered with moss, slimy green, carpeting the small rocks on either side of the path we walk. It is early morning, 9:00 a.m., and this is our daily ritual. We walk from the dock at the end of the street to the small store at the beach, where I will get a Goody Bar or a Creamsicle. This is 1960. This is no convenience store, but a small, family-owned shop with wooden floors and a stale smell. I love my father. Every morning I wait for the walk, the time when it is just him and me. No world. No one else. We will walk down to the end of Shady Lane and it is just twenty paces until I start to feel free of the cottage we share with my cousins, my mother and sister, my aunts and uncles. Where we sleep four to a bed, all we can afford for one week a year, it is our vacation, the best a working-class household can muster. We hold hands during the one-mile walk and I hold my breath to escape the stink of rotting wood, lumps of seaweed, dead fish floating near the shore. Still, there is the terrible lapping that never stops. I hold my breath for as long as I can, trying to look content and peaceful. Then I turn my head away from the lake, take in one long gulp of air, and resume the holding in. I never tell my father I am doing this. I try to listen well, nod my head, speak in short phrases, keep my eyes straight ahead, and be with my father. There is a lot of silence, which I like. It is absolutely imperative that I don't let my father know how much I hate the smell of this lake, I am afraid we will never take this walk again, that our time will be gone forever. This is my father, my ally, and still the underpinnings of this fear are tremendous.

In that isolated mile of time

In that isolated mile of time, my father has become my ally, my grounding force. He sees me in a way no one does. He does not try to change me. As we walk, I know that the end of this path is coming. I can't accept its ending. I want the world to be me and my father, no one else. As we walk past other cottages, I wonder what the families are doing inside? Are their children real? Do they all look alike? We come out into the open and the terrible lapping stops. But the terrible openness begins. Who will know that I am not real? Can they tell with one glance? Is my father afraid too? I don't think so. Will I do something wrong that will give me away?

Like a mack truck on a dark interstate

Like a Mack truck on a dark interstate, the life of the untold story bears down on the heart of the child—the pressure felt with no explanation, the no belonging, no resembling, the no imprinting of the adopted child living in a dead landscape where no story keeps hers alive.

I am the adopted child, the ghost in the story. I need to remain visible in an acceptable way, or all bets are off. I need to appear as a biological child might appear, which of course is no one way. This is part of the terror of the child's story: she is trying to build a right way to be—out of nothing—out of watching others, trying to figure out what it is they are doing to try to make themselves acceptable children.

The adopted child monitors these patterns with the hypervigilance of a prisoner, out of a relentless sense of the provisional. The child looks up at the soft red face of the father, it is too dangerous to breathe in and out, the father taking the child's hand by the lake, the incomprehensible importance of the single gesture, the small waves—no, not waves, but rolls of water hitting the sidewall of the path they're on. I'm looking at my father's soft red face. I smile with my breath held:

We are happy, happy in the terrible passage of time. How could I freeze this moment—me and him forever? No one else, no one in. Fish heads, planks of wood, everything oily and

*saturated, things cast off in the hungry lake. Did he think I
was being too quiet?*

*Give me the terrible water, the gulping of air—you can keep
the world, with its families, its horribly solid shapes—I'll be the
ghost walking into the woods.*

three

the real and the unreal, glistening

> When foreground and background share a single
> plane like this, the meaning is clear: the land is a
> part of her. Where does it end and she begin?
> —Joni Mitchell

Mother of Blood

Mother of Blood, Mother of Skin, I don't know whose life I'm in: Adopted's not chosen but plucked from some womb/and still I'm the wren on the porch looking in.

Did anyone's heart have to break just to make me? And which is the place that holds me to the ground? I'm writing these lines, I'm shooting for the wild heart of accident and still you have no face/mother/4:00 a.m. I'm rabid with my own heart/ empty & full with the shape of your face/I'm starving, mother, in my no/story, speaking to the no/one of you.

Do you know the yellow scarf of grief, how it hangs or saves you? It could come tonight/ten years from now on any street: I walk in the still/born night and there you are: air packed tight with bone/hair/your hands first touching me/I twirl to the huge zero of you, into all your faces lining my dreams like barnacles/now we're beyond the lump in the throat to the shaking at night till my lover stops me—nothing wrong—my bones shaking yesterday/back to today, this time worse, this time you:

Mother of Blood feeding the tremor, mother of rupture, bruise & shudder; Phantom; Specter; Apparition; Fracture & hoard; Quake & splinter. Just fill the "never" of looking like anyone. Give me the story, broken & beautiful: give me the body parts, detailed & sweet, till there is nothing, nothing left faceless.

Tonight I would say: *Tell me what the air felt like the last day you held me, the snatch of lilacs that brushed the dormer at the foundling home, how its sweetness hung thick in the air like a ticket out, all the hands, the boys' hands you'd lose yourself in those nights you'd sneak out, the magnolia talc and rosewater you'd smooth on your skin, trying to make one summer night last a year. How much you lost. When our skin finally touched, didn't you know you were home? Tell me: What happens to the body when you hand your child over—does it shake—or recoil into snake?*

Mother of Blood, purging its young; Mother of Skin, Guardian of Scars: See Flush for atonement; see Purify for evacuation, see Exile, Expel, see free and clear.

Tonight I'll tell you the lie of the story: *It was sky-blue. A sitting room with one rocking chair and your hands, large and soft, cupping my head of no hair. And every time you whispered, your voice covered me like a warm stream and no one else was alive or dead. And when you whispered goodbye, it sounded like every other word and that warmth never happened again. Then there was nothing, then nothing, and nothing for a very long time.*

An infant stream is a small, gathering watercourse

> An infant stream is a small, gathering watercourse
> at the very upper reaches of a watershed. Such
> a stream has only begun its erosive mission of
> redistributing the materials of the land downhill.
> In heavy rains, the flow in embryonic rivulets
> grows from a trickle to a wash.
>   —Robert Michael Pyle

The ivy green couch grows rabid in the basement. With patterns too close together, the 1950s embossed leaves the only witnesses when my sister tells me that our adopted parents are not our friends, they are not to be trusted. I am eight years old when she says they are our enemies, people who have stolen us from our real parents. From now on, she says, we have to lie to them about everything. I cry into the green couch—no, I don't want to lie. Shut up, she says—it's the only way to survive. Five years older than me and adopted from another family, she would grow to tower over me at five-foot-ten. We look nothing alike, her hair burns red and her eyes brown. Next to her, my blonde hair, green eyes, and five-foot-three frame give us nothing in common—except our life and death battle.

The real and the unreal, glistening

The real and the unreal, glistening. This is what my sister taught me. Adopted from another place, she was real and unreal, and I idolized her. We shouldered through the ghost-lands together, the only people we knew who understood this strange life of adoption. In the midst of the trauma, the dislocation of our "unreal" lives, I lived the fantasy and magic of the ghost kingdom through my sister:

"Adoptees live their everyday experience in their 'pretend' family and another in the 'time tunnel' of the Ghost Kingdom they share with the idealized and denigrated birth parents. If we can grasp the unreality of the realm wherein adoptees perceive their most real selves to reside, we will understand the adopted person's own sense of unreality and how, at any age, conscious thoughts of reunion with the birth mother back in the womb, which the Ghost Kingdom represents, can bring with them terrifying images of disintegration into nothingness." (Lifton)

My sister was magical with her bigger-than-life pink lips, dancing in tight pants to 45's in the tiled working-class basement. Her hair was teased up high—red—and she snuck cigarettes and bourbon at every turn. As a child, I wanted to be her—I wanted her boyfriends and her wild and runaway adventures. I was the ghost explorer looking for the golden answer, my holy grail. I made my choice—I chose my sister early. As children, we were our own army, but we were both terribly lost and broken. We didn't share blood, but we moved through this shattered growing up time together.

My sister is moving in me again

my sister is moving in me again   with her long   arms
and legs   moving to tell me   she's still here   inside my
body   along with fireballs   free-roaming breath some
days she's a tanker truck   magnetic   gleaming down
my highways some days   an ocean liner   splitting
the dark waters   today   my sister's particular beauty
rocks the house   back to 1965   wearing pink-pink-
caked-on lipstick   tight pants teased-up-Ann-Margaret
hair   could've been   anyone's sister and was   adopted
from another place   she raised me up   taught   me
the necessary things: how to mix   water with
bourbon in the picture-frame bar   how to mix   the
real and the unreal   and make it glisten   sea of
submerged heartache   great blanket of sea: seamount
sweptback   from the guyot to the springboard   sluice
railbed   heart of copper field   nightshade   when
she hid her arsonist boyfriend   in the basement closet
(when the cops came looking for him)   she taught me
the power of a lie: *no, I haven't seen him   no, not since
yesterday*   she taught me to be visible   then follow the
circle down: ball bearings axehandles   fields of snakes
hot spur of escape   when she ran downstairs to tip
him off: *now! through the backyards   they won't look
there*   she gave and gave   early lessons in desire   her
and her dark-haired muscle boy   on the rock   behind
the shopping center   me the lookout   air thick with

everything coming   his thin t-shirt   i watched their
mouths: |torrential| everything i wanted   moving
through them   today I name the lasting roads: *artery*
toll road   road of disguise   she taught me imprisonment
not being a rat: I took to the heat   like a dog to an
electric fence   don't go past   the edge of the   yard
two girls blank from no beginnings   in combat   so tall
the only way to beat her   was to scissor her between my
thick legs   and squeeze   tonight   the house humming
her particular beauty: lack of compromise   she
grabbed the nail scissors   stabbed me: *sea of the head*
thrown back   she, later dancing to loud music   said:
do it like this, don't listen   to what they tell you   sea we
never shared   blood sea

A river or stream seeks comfort over its own bed

> A river or stream seeks comfort over its own bed. It scours its channel, wears down obstacles, carries sand grains and boulders drawn from its outback, runs its course with the sheer weight of its will. A graded stream is a somewhat theoretical stream—explained by fluid mechanics, felt as mystery.
> —Ellen Meloy

My adopted mother and I never had one good moment. Not one real deep connecting moment. What I never forgot: to watch and weigh, to see how she was standing. With her stiff spine, ready to come towards me? Where was the dark salmon-colored hairbrush with its unforgiving bristles? I never forgot to look around the room and see if anyone was around to see, she never wanted witnesses. How to leave, tell her I had homework to do? Always check her eyes, but I knew what I would see in them: nothing.

For many years, I felt it was my fault, my fault—whoever had me, gave me away for good reason. Just put me somewhere, I decided, since I didn't know any story. Maybe on the street, maybe like in the movies, or like I had seen other babies—wrapped in a sweet pink blanket—but mine was dirty, maybe ripped, maybe she didn't have money, nowhere to put me, just running the streets one morning and no one around so she said: *here.*

And then kept running, maybe she was on her way to Mass, maybe to ask for forgiveness, because she didn't mean it, she couldn't do anything else—but then maybe she took one look at me and said, *ugly,* said *isn't what I wanted, too small, not how I imagined*—and then I look up and see my adopted mother standing there—and I know I'm not what she

wanted, not how she imagined. I know this every minute of every day through ten thousand gestures and postures and breathings and bowed head and dead eyes. I know it when she brushes my hair every morning with the dark salmon-colored brush. It is just me and her. No one is here to see. No one can ever save me from this.

the brushing

it is what we do and i hate it. she kneels in front of me i am six. she holds up the dark salmon-colored hairbrush with black bristles. full of her black hair, full of my sister's red hair. stand still she says, but she says it in this hissing way, she is disgusted with me every day, i don't do things the way she wants and all i want to do is get out of there before she gets close two inches from my face her breath is always hot and sour coming straight at me her mouth open with the bobby pins in her teeth i think a moth will fly out of there i want something to fly out of there and save me pick me up and fly me away so i never never have to see her again but then they would have to take my father too and i love him he is so kind and I can't tell him about the brushing and her breath because he would say she's just getting you ready for school but i know this is not just that this is her hating me and wishing i would be cute and cuddly but i don't want her to touch me i don't want her to ever touch me her touch is like something bad put on you like a cover and then you can't breathe and i know she doesn't want to touch me but does it in front of people to make them think she does it other times but only to hit she hits us when we're in bed but i don't mind that since i'm with my sister and it doesn't really hurt what i mind is when it is just her and me and she is too close just breathing and wishing i was somebody else i hold my breath so i don't have to smell her i close my eyes and pretend i am somewhere else down at the dock by the lake with my *girlfriend patty and there is air fresh air and a horizon a place to travel to*

The Pedophile and the Adoptive Mother Speak

The pedophile and the adoptive mother speak in similar ways.

The sentences that an adoptive mother should never say to her adopted child:

Don't worry, I'm your mother now. Your mother's here. I'm your mother and I love you.

They have a similar ring to the pedophile's words: *Over here, I have a present for you.*

This is enticement under false pretenses: *your mother now.* At stake in both instances: erasure of the self as the perpetrator represents the rules of the game, but leaves out the truth: *I'm not who I say I am.* Lying about essential truths is not a small detail. Say it true:

I purchased you through the court system, the adoption agency, the black market, a woman my sister knows, etc. etc. I paid good money for you.

The sentences an adoptive mother needs to say to her adopted child:

I can never be your mother. I can never fill that hole. I'm sorry for your loss.

This has a similar ring to what is said at someone's dying, and there has been a death.

A death of a person's beginnings, identity, relationship to and location in the world. This death can never be healed and should never be erased. Would you ever say: *Oh, Uncle Larry didn't die—this guy's your Uncle Larry now.*

He made a bunker for me

He made a bunker for me. My adoptive father, he somehow knew I needed a place to be, he built a forty-by-forty plywood platform in the attic. I would climb the ladder daily—this is where I kept myself with books he bought—a lamp, some food, and a trap door closed behind me in the blue light.

Bringing home baby

Bringing Home Baby was the name of the book. I was six years old and outside playing. I remember my mother calling me in and giving me this hardcover, sea-green book with a picture of a mother in a dress, a father in a suit, and they were on their way somewhere, pushing a baby carriage. My mother told me that I was adopted and to read it. We were in the bedroom, and I said okay, then set it on the bed, and went back outside to play. It didn't really register that much with me then—it couldn't register. It was too large, I was too small, and I couldn't really imagine what she was telling me. I don't think that we ever talked about it again, but there are years and years of my childhood that I don't remember.

This is the splitting that happens with adoptees at an early age. In *Journey of the Adopted Self*, Betty Jean Lifton states: "Implicit in the parents' loving message to the child is: 'We will love you as our own unconditionally—under the condition that you pretend that you are really our own.' The child is being asked to collude in the fiction that these are his only parents and to accept that his birth heritage is disposable."

I was raised in the 1950s, in the era of "closed" adoptions—meaning that the adopted child had no access to her name, her background, medical records, etc. My birth certificate lists my name as Janet Patrice Beatty—with no other information. It took me years to get a *preamended* birth certificate—after research and many calls and letters to the Bureau of Vital Statistics. They refused my requests. Finally, I reached a woman who wanted to help me, someone who went outside the parameters of her job and told me who to contact and what language to use.

I was living in an apartment in Squirrel Hill in Pittsburgh when the preamended birth certificate arrived in the mail. In the red lake of my childhood, I had two mothers: mother of blood and mother of stone. Strangely enough, I was living with two women—a rabid Christian and a hooker: one who read the Bible aloud in the dining room; another a graduate student from California who charged men for sex as a way to pay off her student loans. The Christian posted schedules for cleaning and invited me to read the Bible with her. We fought regularly. It took me a while to realize that the men visiting my other roommate were tricks. I worked as a waitress at O'Rourkes and was deep into my addiction to drugs and alcohol. I didn't mind the men coming through the apartment, but the Bible and the cleaning schedule disturbed me.

The names arrived. So strange and terrifying to find out my blood from a single piece of paper: My name: Patrice Staiger. Mother: Dorothy Staiger. Father: Tim Curran. I would later find out that this preamended birth certificate wasn't accurate either.

four

something living

Suddenly you'll remember life as something living
rather than something that was lived.

—Michael Klein

I was wordless, airless, buried
with hundreds of others, small broken birds,
little Bastards.

—Jean O'Brien

The two countercurrents rip along

> The two countercurrents rip along each other, separated by a purgatory fault that can surge several feet high. A boat on the eddy side of the fence may be looking 'uphill' into the main flow, perhaps in the precarious state of either being eddied out or made an eddy prisoner.
>
> —Ellen Meloy

I had the dream about the white bars again. Metal bars. White metal bars of a crib in a roomful of cribs. I don't know if I remember people. But someone came. Who was it? In the dream—strange light, not very bright—and lots of shadow. Movement.

I wrote a poem about nuns surrounding babies in cribs before I knew about the Sisters of Charity handling my adoption. Before I knew that I was born in Roselia Asylum and Maternity Hospital on Cliff and Manilla Streets. How is that possible?

I went to see Roselia, but it had since moved to Bedford Avenue in the Hill District of Pittsburgh—then closed down and became a refuge for homeless men: St. Joseph's House of Hospitality.

When I looked up Roselia, here's what I found:

Black and white photos. A room full of white metal cribs. Nuns in white apron-like habits lifting up babies from the cribs.

Sisters M. Camillus Erb (left) and Grace Hayes
Roselia nursery, 1957

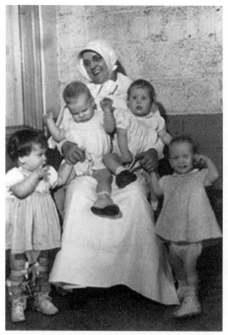

Sister Mary Kieran Beyer keeps close watch over
her wards
(Roselia ca. 1948)

moving picture orphanage

i imagine the crosscut wind i was born in the howling came
first, then a body behind

white bars, cast-iron 1950s, the cribs lined up like a made-
for-tv movie

white bars in a metal crib—whose idea was that?

then nothing, no one but the women in long robes their
nightmarish bending

over/they're coming/who are they/in this filmstrip of birth
someone is crying, smells

of shit, flies around the bottle dish

if it's science fiction, then give me the gold kimono, the glow-
ing light, not this whitewash

blight: no body to be laid on/to be put next to—no white-
horse savior coming/

She only tried a little, unwound the coat hanger and put it inside her

She only tried a little, unwound the coat hanger and put it inside her. There was a lot of blood, he said. When my birth-mother tried to give herself an abortion, he said that she used a coat hanger to try to cause a "miscarriage." She was desperate, he said, and panicking about being pregnant and what would she do, she had no money, couldn't raise a baby.

But who was he? I didn't trust him, his name was on my birth certificate, but who was he, really? He said: *She only tried a little, unwound the coat hanger and put it inside her.* Was he there? He said she pushed inside with it a few times, and the bleeding started, and then she stopped. There was a lot of blood, he said, and she thought that she would "miscarry," but it never happened. After that, she hid herself in the up-stairs bedroom and waited.

I never asked her about that story. But I wondered if it was true. I believe it is, and in thinking about it, I struggled to imagine what it might have felt like from the inside of her body.

An abortion attempt by my mother

Rolling side to side in my warm mother, the juices of life pulsing through my veined skin, wild juices of calves' tongues and loose stretchy kid skin like young gray wrens.

I drink unborn water in the Garfield back room in the dark while my mother cries.

The prodding of wolves' teeth, eyes red and ailing, the shaking of orange clay and cracked slate, the loosening, exposing the underground creatures to full sky, the greased worms are screaming, the dead moles stay dead.

This is the feeling.

I didn't come inside her

I didn't come inside her. That's what he said when I called.

A storm beach is a paradoxical feature

> A storm beach is a paradoxical feature of the
> coast, a barrier of gravel, rocks, shingle, even
> boulders, piled up by extreme storm waves
> behind the normal margin of the beach and
> acting as a shield or curtain wall against all but
> the most violent later storms.
>
> —Robert Morgan

Many adopted children have nightmares, often repeating ones about kidnapping, being "stolen" from their beds. Many adoptees have great fear of being "sent back" to wherever they came from, fear of not being "good enough" to stay with the adopted parents.

My recurring nightmare was of an overheard conversation:

My mother and sister are in the bathroom, whispering.
  They are saying: we can't keep her, we have to give her back.
  Then:
  It's too late, they're never going to take her back now,
  we have to kill her.
  I think it's the only way.
  We have to do it soon, before her father finds out—
  he'll try to stop us.
  Okay, tonight.
  In the dream, they each have knives. They are coming
  out of the bathroom towards my bedroom. That's when
  I would wake up.

My white quilted bedspread with green and pink stitching, my sister next to me in bed—was she asleep? Had she just returned to bed after plotting with my adoptive mother? Years later, in a hotel room in New Orleans, I had the dream again, and it took me down trembling into the red lake of my past. I know the terror. In the body of my young self, I knew I couldn't tell anyone about the dream. If I couldn't trust my adopted mother and sister, then who would believe me?

Something made me turn

Something made me turn to look at a woman across the room. Lunch shift at O'Rourkes, dining room full. Wasn't even my section. I turned to see two women sitting at a window table. I can't explain this. I knew that one of the women was my aunt. I looked around at my tables, looked to see where my manager was.

Waiting on my tables, delivering food, I kept looking over at her. A panic set in. I had to do it. I walked out of the kitchen with plates of burgers and fries lining my arms, saw her paying her tab at the bar. I delivered the food and walked over to her, not knowing what I was going to say, but knowing I had to go. I didn't even know if I had an aunt, but I knew this was her.

"Hi," I said.

She turned around, her face about twelve inches from mine. It was her, she had the same fair skin as my birthmother, similar features and light eyes.

"Yes?" she said.

I knew I had to cut to the chase:

"Do you know a woman named Dorothy?" I said (my birthmother's name).

A strange thing happened, her countenance totally changed. Her face seemed to drain of the blood that I was sure we shared. Her eyes looked hard at me, like a laser, and she was tough and serious for a quick moment. She knew something.

"No, no, I don't," she said, fumbling with her purse.

Then, she shifted again, her face became blank, neutral—almost like putting on a coat. She looked over her shoulder. Her friend was ready to leave.

"I have to go," she said.

She looked at me again and said, "I did have a sister named Dorothy, but she died."

I looked at her, and I'm sure that my face changed also, that my eyes widened, as if to say, *Really, that's what you're going to say?*

"Okay," I said, and that was it.

The earth shifted in the bar that day, in the middle of life, the middle of commerce—eating, paying, staying alive. I can't explain any of it, but my body took me out of the moment and thrust me into another life. It was the red sugar, the blood that schooled me, the great mystery. I don't know her name, never saw her again, but at a later meeting with my birthmother, I relayed the story. She got the same look of terror/recognition on her face and said that yes, she does have a sister, but no—that couldn't—that couldn't have possibly been her.

Red Sugar

> You walk inside yourself on roads and ropes
> of blood vessels and tendons, you walk inside
> yourself and eat weather
>
> —Gretel Ehrlich

When I was young, I was a comet with an unending shimmering tail, and I flew over the brokenness below that was my life. I didn't know until I was twelve that we carry other bodies inside us. Not babies, but bodies of blood that speak to us in plutonic languages of pith and serum. When I was six, there was a man in the woods, naked. I didn't know him, but I knew he was a wrong kind of man/so I ran. With my inside body I see his skinny white bones and curled mouth, he looks like sickness and it's the body inside me that's running, my red sugar body that shows me the brutal road to love, the one good man, the one song I can keep as mine. I heard it once when I was waitressing, something made me turn my head, made me swivel to look at a woman across the room, wasn't even my station, but the red sugar said, go. When I saw her up close, I knew she was blood. I can't explain this—

I said, Do you know a woman named Dorothy? Her face was pale, she said, No—in that hard way. Maybe her red sugar told her to run—but before she left, she grabbed my arm, said, I did have a sister named Dorothy, but she died. Two inches away from her dyed blonde hair, I said, okay, but both our inside bodies knew she was lying. Some people call it eating weather—the way you swallow what you know, but keep it—later it rises like a storm from another world, reptilian and hungry. It's the thickness that drives us and stains us, the not asking/ just coming/the cunt alive and jewel-like/the uncut garnet and the lava flow/it's barbarism/bloodletting/the most liquid part of us/spilling/spreading/the granular red sea of sap and gore/ sinking/moving forward at the same time/slippery/red containing blue/it's the sweet, deep inside of the body.

five

river of sight

Every bad situation is a blues song waiting to happen.

—Amy Winehouse

Where birds are singing. Or unsinging if that's your experience.

—Diane Glancy

The curtain wall

The curtain wall took years to form.

> There is no more consequential step than
> abandoning the real self.
>
> —Karen Horney

As a very young child, around the age of six, seven, eight—my terror seemed to grow. Some incidents had occurred in the neighborhood, with a man exposing himself to me and some other children. Then some men in a white car pulled up in front of my house and asked me to get in. I didn't, but I thought: *it's me they want. They know where I live.* I didn't tell my parents. Nothing felt like a safe thing to do.

This sense of not feeling safe is common with adoptees. In *Journey of the Adopted Self,* Betty Jean Lifton says: "The child forced to give up the real self cannot develop feelings of belonging. There is instead a feeling of basic anxiety, of being isolated and helpless. Adopted children often try to shut out the subject of adoption. This means that they must separate one part of the self from the rest of the self—a pattern known as dissociation, disavowal, numbing, or splitting."

Things got worse when I didn't tell anyone about what was happening. I was in a state of panic. I'm not sure at what point I started hiding in the attic. I would get a ladder, ask my adopted dad (who was my ally) to move aside the wooden hatch and then I'd climb inside. I took a small lamp and some books to read. This should have been a clue to my parents that I needed therapy, but it was the 1950s, early sixties, and there was significant stigma attached to getting help.

The separation of the attic gave me great comfort. I felt safe up there, and more importantly, could escape into reading, where I didn't exist—and where none of this "family" and fear existed. Over time, my father saw me in some way—he built a platform for me to sit on (this was not a finished attic, just boxes and two-by-fours to balance on. There was a lot of that pink insulation, most likely asbestos). On that sheet of three-foot-square plywood: one small lamp, a stack of books, a bag of caramels. A folded towel to sit on. The air was thick up there, a place to dream of other worlds and ideas. A place that was *mine*. My father started to buy books for me—I was reading *The Hardy Boys*, since I hated Nancy Drew and her dresses and what seemed like less interesting adventures. My father helped to keep me sane and alive, and I was grateful for him every day.

I didn't feel safe at night. I needed cover, protection. I made a sleeping bag out of two pillowcases, cut and sewed it together myself. It was big enough to cover me. I crawled into it every night. It didn't stop the nightmares, but it helped. I could pretend that I was somewhere else, on a camping trip. Not in the woods, but in another world.

When I was eleven, there was a man following me in downtown Pittsburgh, and I couldn't shake him. When I would go into a store, so would he. He got on the escalator behind me in Gimbels and shoved his knee between my legs. When I got off that escalator, I quickly looked around for an ally—the woman poking through the sales piles? No.

The salesclerk, she might be able to get someone to help me. I walked toward her, and she walked away. I felt alone. He was looking at me from across the room. I started running.

Running up the moving steps, running onto the street, never looking back, running to my bus. He was gone.

Again, I didn't tell anyone. I didn't know who I could trust. As an adoptee, I was too afraid of "ruining" the one good relationship I had, with my father. What if he didn't believe me, thought it was my fault?

Shortly after that, a peeping tom started coming to our house. The first time, I was in the living room with my family, and I saw a face at the small window in the front door. I screamed. *There's someone there*, I said. *Don't be ridiculous*, my mother said. My father got up and opened the door. There was no one there. *Maybe you saw a shadow*, he said.

Weeks later, I was home alone. My sister was over at a friend's house, my parents most likely at my aunt's house up the street. I was in my bedroom and heard a scraping sound.

I didn't know what it was at first. The scraping continued, like something against rock.

I looked up and saw a man's face at my window—I screamed and yanked the curtains shut. The scraping stayed. I realized it was the ladder moving back and forth against the bricks of the house. Back and forth. Then more movement. I realized years later that he was jerking off on the ladder. It was a second floor window. He had brought a ladder, an extension ladder. He really wanted to get to that window, to get to me.

I don't have any memory of that night, what happened after. It's a blank. I don't remember my parents coming home. But I did tell them what happened. They didn't believe me. *No one would bring an extension ladder to look in your window*, they said. Even my dad thought this was far-fetched. My mother: *You're making it up. That's ridiculous. No one would do that.* It was my first time telling them of this terror, and my last time. I felt like someone was stalking me. Was it the same man from the car? Why did they want me?

About a week later, he came back. He was bold. He came to the front door window—and this time, I yelled, *He's there!* My dad jumped up, threw open the door and grabbed for him. He chased him through the yard, around the back, and lost him. The police came and looked for him. They told us to take it seriously. I told them about the ladder, the second-story window. They believed me. I was grateful that it became real to everyone. That finally, everyone saw that there was someone after me.

My dad installed frosted glass in the front windows. I pinned my drapes shut permanently. Another sign that I needed some help. This was the curtain wall that would keep me safe from the faces, the man coming after me. I made sure that all the windows were locked, all the time. The curtain wall would keep his face away. Nothing could stop the scraping in my dreams, in my body.

Dead babies

Dead babies seemed to be the only answer. What to do with these dolls?

> Adult adoptees often speak as if they have split
> off a part of the self back in those preverbal days:
> they speak of feeling unborn, having a dead space
> in the center like a hollow core, of carrying a
> "dead baby inside."
> —Betty Jean Lifton

One of the worst parts: she couldn't run. Her moveable arms and legs were stiff: only moveable at the control of someone else. Just like me, a prisoner. She had to go. I decided to hang and bury her.

I was given two dolls as a child. The first one was nondescript, characterless. Kind of large, about two feet high, with blonde hair sticking out of the many-patterned holes in her head. The color of her skin was pink-white, not a real color. She was fake, like me—not a real girl. Her blue eyes disturbed me in their perfection. The edge of the iris read almost as silver—cold, overly precise in their blinking. Even more disturbing, the blue bows on the side of her head: diminutive, unremarkable. Predictably, she wore a blue dress. Kind of jumper-like. The kind a good girl would wear on her way to school. I hated her.

I found a piece of rope in the garage, cut it with scissors for the right length. Wound it around her pink neck and knotted it. I hung her from the wooden crossbar in my closet. Unsure as to how long it would take to kill her, I let her hang for weeks behind my sister's clothes on the left side of the closet. I wanted it permanent. I wanted her gone.

Every so often, I would check on her to see if she was still there. I knew nothing about babies. For all I knew, she could disappear, like me, and end up in the hands of another girl. Even though I killed her, I wanted her to stay.

Afterwards, I cut her down, stuffed her headfirst into a pile of clothes on the floor of the closet. Covered her with books and shoes for final burial. No one would find her.

My second doll was Chatty Cathy. She was more frightening than the first one, because she was trying to speak. Even larger than Doll #1, Chatty was about three feet high in a royal blue dress. Again, blonde hair and blue eyes. She could have been a sister of the first doll, they shared similar features. White cotton anklets, miniature black patent shoes. A white ring protruded from her back—so humans could make her speak. This control again, making your "doll" be what you wanted, do what you wanted. I don't know if I consciously made this connection to adoption, but I knew it was all wrong.

Chatty was more produced, more sophisticated than Doll #1—no patterns of holes for her yellow strings of hair, Chatty's hair was springy, you could style it. If you liked that kind of thing. Her marble-y eyes seemed to roll back into her head, making this terrible clunking sound. But we had something in common: we were alien children, not like the others. When I pulled the ring in her back, a sickly squeak voice: *My name is Chatty, what's yours?* or *Let's be friends.* Fat chance, I thought—your days are numbered. I pulled and pulled the ring, trying to break her, make her forget what she was saying. She kept talking. This would have to be a different murder. I had to make sure that she could never speak again.

I decided on drowning. I went to the garage and found a galvanized steel tub, which held the garden hose. This operation took some time, as I pulled the hose out, dragged the tub to the stationery tubs in the basement. How would I be able to lift this? I dragged it back to the garage, reconnected the garden hose, and turned on the water. I would kill her in the garage. This was not a game, but very serious to me. Chatty felt like a threat to me, everything I hated. I wanted to make it so that she could no longer function.

When the tub was full, I grabbed Chatty, pushed her under, and held. She would have to stay submerged for a while. I waited. Longer. When I finally brought her up, I tested: pull the string and—nothing. Just the sound of the string coming out of her body, the dull, scraping sound. I took the body, wrapped it in a blanket. Took her upstairs for burial under the useless dresses in the closet. She would never bother me again.

A particularly chaotic type of gaping

> A particularly chaotic type of gaping
> river hole, a cauldron, is characterized by "big,
> squirrelly, boily water" . . . they sometimes produce
> ferocious hydraulics—violent whirlpools, geysers,
> and suddenly collapsing haystacks of white water.
> —Terry Tempest Williams

Project 60 (1976)—I was hired as a social worker for a pilot project, Project 60, at Moundsville Penitentiary in West Virginia, an ancient maximum security prison. My job: to work with men sixty years and older who had been in prison all their lives. I would make a life plan with them for when they were released. I was twenty-four years old.

As a bastard, I felt a kinship to prisoners. They couldn't move about the world as they wanted, their histories were not valued. In college, I joined the Prison Reform Task Force on campus. I read about the wrongly accused, devoured the story of George Jackson and the Soledad Brothers. I idolized Angela Davis and her bravery. I was beyond naïve.

The first day, I knew I was in over my head. Walking past the yard in my summer dress, with long blonde hair, I've never felt that feeling before or since—that feeling of being *intensely looked at* by a group of men. Of course, I've been looked at by men before, but this had a different quality to it. I could feel the prolonged look in my body, if that makes sense. The next day I pulled my hair back, put on some glasses, and wore dress pants. The walk past the yard wasn't much better.

But when I met my clients in the Old Men's Colony, I liked them. They seemed like grandfathers—friendly, quiet, full of stories, and ready for release. As part of my job, I read their files in the prison office, and that's when the structures began to collapse. The distance between my perceptions of them and their crimes, their brutal backgrounds, was staggering. It was like a huge wall of water washing over me.

Prior to my job at the prison, I had worked as a counselor at Allegheny Women's Center, an abortion clinic in Pittsburgh. I thought that I could handle tough, emotional situations. My training as a social worker couldn't help me in prison. What terrified me the most was not the brutality of the crimes that these men were convicted of—it was how they appeared. My perceptions were useless in prison—these men were professionals. Even after I had read the files, when I talked with them again, they seemed like nice guys. Nice guys who had murdered young children, sodomized them and dumped them under a tree.

Maybe some of them were wrongly convicted. But who was who?

I was terrified. As an adoptee, one of the toughest things is the idea of shifting identities. No one is who they say they are: the adopted parents are masquerading as the "real" parents, the "real parents" don't seem to exist, the adoptee's story is invisible, and the adoptee herself is operating under an alias. It's essential to the adoptee to be able to cut through the bullshit in life and find what seems like the "truth." Deception rings like a violence to the adoptee.

So, when I found myself in maximum security with so much brutality that appeared as friendliness, I was in trouble. I should have expected deception, violence, and brutality in prison, yes—but what I didn't expect was that I couldn't see it for what it was.

Predictably, I didn't last long. One of my clients murdered another one of my clients in the Old Men's Colony. No one knew who did it. After that, when I talked with one of the men, I would scrutinize his facial movement, his eyes, the way he was standing—to try to break the code: *was he the killer?* I couldn't handle it, and realized that I didn't want to help the men who were to be released. What if I was helping the man who killed my client? I left that job more wary than when I went into it. Talking about prison reform and working in the prisons were two different things. I started to feel, very acutely, some of my limitations.

Penitentiary

My name is Gale, you whisper. I step back, you step forward. I'm inches from your pasty skin, your ice-blue eyes. *Where you from?*

    Philadelphia, I lie, in case you remember, in case you ever get out.

    You know I'm lying. You know my working-class shoes, my cheap Lerner's dress, my predictable blonde hair. You're sixty-five/I'm twenty-three in the old men's colony.

Warden says:
    Don't worry, Gale never speaks above a whisper to anyone.

I get to know you in the scan & rattle of facts in your file:
    Four years old beaten & molested/State Children's Home till sixteen/convicted at eighteen/sodomy of minor/victims three to eight years/convicted/murder first degree/neighbor boy raped & strangled in bushes behind home

The boy/in the bushes/his tiny body/what/did you whisper/ when you strapped/his neck down?

The next time I see you/day after lockdown/one of my clients/ one of your friends/raped & strangled/tangled in bedsheets/ belt cinched around his neck/in his cell/
    Who do you think did it? you ask as you walk up behind me.

I turn to see your eyes, everything I'm afraid of: the salesman
in the five & ten his misshapen head, eyes darting like stray
bullets; the old man downtown who followed my Catholic
girl uniform, shoved his knee between my legs; the man who
put the ladder to my window & masturbated on the brick/
sperm on the mortar/sperm on the mortar/

I don't want to help you/I don't want to look/knowing you
were murdered/as a small child/poor small boy with no heart/

I'm looking for the name/of the first/person who hurt a child/

I was born with chances/were you born with none—
still I close my heart:

When I tell the warden I don't want to help you/when I pull
my hair back/when I keep my eyes down/when I quit my job/
when I see you again & again in my dreams, a ghost plays a
white fiddle: all our sins over & over in a thin whine.

six

Photos

The body will record the events
and the child will look like what happened.
—Sharon Doubiago

Roselia Asylum and Maternity Hospital, ca. 1952
Cliff and Manilla Streets in the Hill District
Pittsburgh, Pennsylvania

The Playroom
Roselia Asylum and Maternity Hospital, ca. 1950
Cliff and Manilla Streets in the Hill District
Pittsburgh, Pennsylvania

"Wild Bill" Ezinicki
Right Wing, Toronto Maple Leafs, 1944–1950
Winner of three Stanley Cups
Scored eighty-four goals, 113 assists in 408 career National Hockey
League games

"Wild Bill" Ezinicki
Right Wing, Boston Bruins
1950–51, 1951–52

Dorothy Staiger, 1947
Peabody High School
Pittsburgh, Pennsylvania

Dorothy Staiger
September, 2014

seven

the machine

The machine conceals the machinations.
> —Ursula K. Le Guin

I think there is choice possible at any moment to us,
as long as we live. But there is no sacrifice. There is
a choice, and the rest falls away. Second choice does
not exist. Beware of those who talk about sacrifice.
> —Muriel Rukeyser

1982, the call

1982, the call I was afraid to make. The name on my birth certificate was kind of common—Tim Curran. About ten of them in the Pittsburgh phone book, was he even still living here? My only plan: to call and say, "Your name is on my birth certificate. Did you have a daughter in 1952?" I realized that I might be calling someone who didn't want to hear from me. I decided on the Curran who was listed as a restaurant supply business, in large print.

Shaky, I dialed the phone.

"Hello," a voice said.

"Are you Tim Curran?" I said.

"Yes, how can I help you?"

"This is a little strange, but I have a birth certificate here with your name on it."

Nothing. No sound.

"It has your name listed under father, along with Dorothy Staiger under mother, and my name, Patrice Staiger. My adopted name is Jan Beatty."

There's a cough, a pause, throat clearing, and his voice has changed into a fractured, softer voice:

"Ah, I'm at work . . . can I call you back in a few minutes?"

"Okay," I said.

It was shocking to hear his voice, this father—would he call back? Was he trying to escape?

In ten minutes, he called back. A long ten minutes.

He seemed more composed, his voice back to itself: deep and solid:

"Hello?" I said.

"Is this Jane?" he said.

"Jan," I said, "Jan." "Yes, it's me."

"Jan, I'm at work and had to go to another phone."

"I understand." I knew he had to figure out what he was going to say.

He said, "I did know Dorothy, we were boyfriend and girlfriend when I was in college, but I'm not your father."

"Well, why is your name on my birth certificate?"

"It's a long story. We were dating, I was going to school at Pitt . . . this is very personal. I agreed to put my name on the birth certificate so that there could be a name. There was no one else. I was trying to help Dorothy through this tough time."

"I don't get it," I say.

He seems like he's taken this ten minutes to make up a story. I feel like he's patronizing me.

"You have to understand," he says, "it was the early fifties. We were dating, but she wouldn't sleep with me. We would do everything but have sex, but she wouldn't do it.

(I'm thinking, I wouldn't sleep with you either, you sound like a pain in the ass.)

He says, "And then one night, all of a sudden, she wanted to have sex. I was surprised, but I was a young guy, I was gonna go along with it."

I'm saying nothing, feeling like this is incredibly weird to have this old guy tell me this story. I feel no connection with him, this name on my birth certificate.

"Two weeks later, we're at a party, she gets drunk, and starts telling me the truth," he says.
   "About what?" I say.

He seems too certain, too rehearsed, like he's been waiting to tell this story—or maybe he knew this call would come one day.

"She's crying and crying—she told me that she had cheated on me, and found out that she was pregnant. She didn't want to tell me, she wanted to have sex with me and then tell me it was our child. But she couldn't do it. As you can imagine, I was angry. We broke up that night."

"How do you know you're not the father?" I said.
   "She told me that she was already pregnant from this other guy. And besides, I pulled out."
   "What?"
   "I didn't come inside her," he said, "I pulled out."

I couldn't believe that he was telling me details about sex with my birthmother. It seemed sleazy, but I was grateful that he was telling me what might be a true story.

I didn't say anything.

"You know," he said, "if you pull out right before you ejaculate . . ."

"Yeah, yeah, I know," I said, "but sometimes that doesn't really work . . ."

The conversation was getting stranger and stranger. It seemed unreal, just when it was supposed to be "real." What seemed clear was that he wanted to separate himself from the mess of this, the mess of my beginnings.

"Look—it was a hard time for Dorothy. We remained friends, and she didn't have a name to put on the birth certificate. She asked if she could use mine."

I found it hard to believe that a young guy who had been cheated on would step up to put his name down on a legal document.

"Well, what about the other guy?" I said.

"She said he was out of the picture."

I didn't have much more to say, didn't know if I believed him.

He didn't ask about me, who I was, if I had met Dorothy. He wanted to end the conversation.

He said something like, "That's the story."

"Okay," I said, and that was it.

Later, I realized that he ran a million-dollar business, and had a lot at stake in not being my father. I didn't know if I believed him. But, if it wasn't him, who was my father?

The cloak of all cloaks

The cloak of all cloaks, the now it's here, now it isn't routine of all times. The adoption industry has perpetrated one of the great institutional lies: not only did you *not* lose your mother, your story, your beginnings—you are the luckiest of all luckys—you are loved more than the others because you were picked (like the sweetest flower from a blooming garden)—and this magic of your life we will call "chosen baby."

The culture of North America has an obsession with "niceness"—or, more accurately, the appearance of niceness. If North America doesn't want to tell the truth about how bad someone looks in a dress or in that sweater—I can live with that. But when North America systematically erases the history of its citizens and then calls the infant a lucky one, a "chosen" baby, enlisting cooperation by invoking the "sacredness of mother love" (another misrepresentation)—I have to draw a line. It's very clear that we, as citizens of the world, are not supposed to question the idea of motherhood. Motherhood as an invention is sacred ground, not to be made dirty by any sense of what's real.

When will it happen that someone will acknowledge that all women who want to adopt are not wonderful people? That all women who bear their own children are not wonderful people? Can we lose the saint/monster framework once and for all? These are human beings going through trauma and joy and wonder and regret and boredom and hatefulness and confusion and every other human emotion.

Can we just let these women be who they are?
    Flawed humans, just like the rest of us?

Second meeting

Second meeting, July 1987. By this time, I knew where my birthmother lived. I called her and asked to meet with her. My anger had grown. I had been to therapy, I wanted to find out who my father was, and this time I was bent on finding out.

We met at a chain restaurant on the Miracle Mile in Monroeville, PA—her pick. The restaurant was crowded, we both had a drink. She was much more relaxed in this meeting— some crying, but no sobbing and grabbing my arm. This time, she wore a casual dress—it looked like she had just gotten off of work. I wore jeans.

Again, she wanted to know how I was. I told her that I was waitressing and taking classes in writing. I said that I needed to know who my father was—that I knew she didn't want me to find him, but that I had a right to know.

"I can't tell you," she said.
   "Why not," I said.
   "It's just not a good situation," she said.
   "Why?"
   "It was a one-night thing," she said, and started to cry a little.
   This time, I felt stronger. I said, "Look, if you don't know who it is, tell me. I talked to the guy on the birth certificate."
   This shocked her.

"It's not him," she said.

"That's what he said, that you all of a sudden were willing to sleep with him, then you broke down and told him the truth."

"He told you that?" she said.

"He said, 'I didn't come inside her.'"

"Oh my God," she said, "that bastard."

"Yeah," I said.

This felt like our first moment of communication. She sat there for a bit, disturbed by what I had told her.

"I can tell you that he's a hockey player," she said.

"What?"

"Yeah, I used to go to hockey games on Tuesday nights to see him."

"Wow," I said, "this is exciting."

She gave me a tough look, and I said, "I know it's complicated, but it's exciting for me to hear this."

"Look," she said, "I can't tell you his name, but he was a star on the team."

"What team?"

"The Pittsburgh Hornets. That's all I can tell you. I shouldn't have told you that."

"Was he the only star, were there a lot of stars?" I asked.

"He was good," she said. "He was the best."

That's all that she would tell me that night. We met for about an hour. I liked her. She was human and flawed and I felt for the first time that she was beginning to see me as the same. Even though I didn't have a name, I knew I had enough to find him.

eight

the rest falls away

There was but the one place for me, at the juncture
of the public lie and private primal power, lines cut
into silence before I was born.

—Linda McCarriston

If this is sex, it must be Tuesday

So it was every week on a Tuesday, that you and your friend, Ginny, strayed from the dance at St. Anselm's to Duquesne Gardens, feigning interest in hockey, waiting to get laid. I can picture it—you in fake cashmere with pearl buttons, a gabardine skirt that hit you at midcalf, you and Ginny shuffling popcorn till last period, when you'd freshen your lips with TORRID RED for the after-game party at the Webster Hall dorms. After all, these were the Pittsburgh Hornets, this was 1951, and you were a poor Irish girl from Garfield with a hard drive for excitement, and hockey was it, getting crosschecked by the best, having stories to tell in your lean, checkered life, left with no father, a reluctant sister, and a mother who cleaned houses for the rich. So when did I happen, this one-night stand with the MVP after his big, icy win, the second Tuesday in February, or the third? Do you remember the feel of his hands on you? Were they rough, or tender, were they bloody from fighting? And when your belly grew into the body you never wanted, did you curse me, try to cut me? Should I say you did your best, a spare girl from a broken family, or should I say it straight—you wanted it, you took it, like we all do, you lied to save yourself, you gave away part of your heart, you couldn't wish it right.

my home is

my home is   outside the body   in the ditch, dirt
i have no fight with the birthmother—it's the buying/
    co-opting/   erasure/
can't-have-a natural-birth-so-you-buy-a-baby

home: old car graveyards—piles, litters   smashed pancake
cars   haze nothingness   blackbird   horse eating
sagebrush   the wild   the west   never tamed—

my home is the stolen/the violence   the camouflaged
what is hidden from the child   falling down shed   lost
bloodline   old farm tools   wide open dirt   i am a
visitor everywhere

home: provisional   not looking   like anyone   dear
spirit guides: (only the good ones)   help me   carry me
through the land of discarded light signals
elevated highways until   I can get back

A misfit stream is one that is out of proportion to its valley

> A misfit stream is one that is out of proportion to its valley. The reference is usually to a stream significantly smaller than the valley might accommodate. Misfit streams may have lost water to climatic changes, to the capture of their water source by another stream, or to the seepage of water down into the floodplain. They are sometimes found in larger meandering valleys, where they carve new smaller meanders into the alluvium deposits on the valley floor.
>
> —Carolyn Servid

I was the misfit stream, now in search of my birthfather. What valley, what country? In our second meeting, my birthmother said, "I can tell you that he's a hockey player." Astounding. She said he played for the Pittsburgh Hornets, that he was a star. I have no name—but I have this.

I researched the Hornets for the 1951 season since that's when I would have been conceived. *Pittsburgh Post-Gazette* articles, National Hockey League stats. This was precomputers. I called the National Hockey League. I asked who was the star player on the 1951 Hornets? They said, "It's hard to say." *Please don't say that*, I thought. I studied and studied the stats. I thought I knew. I thought it was this guy, Bill Ezinicki. It had to be him.

He played one season for the Hornets, also played for the Toronto Maple Leafs, the Boston Bruins, the New York Rangers. He won three Stanley Cups. Bill Ezinicki was known for his crosschecking and fighting. He had more postseason penalties than any player in history. This sounded like him. He played right-wing, number twelve. In one memorable game, there was a prolonged fight between "Wild Bill" Ezinicki and Detroit Red Wing "Terrible Ted" Lindsay. It ended with nineteen stitches and a broken nose for Ezinicki. On hockeyfights. com, it states: "Although the brawl lasted less than four minutes it has been regarded as one of the most violent in hockey history partly because of the reputation of the warriors."

Ezinicki was so brutal that he had an insurance policy that paid him five dollars per suture, and he collected. He was born in Winnipeg, Manitoba. Canadian. I liked the idea of a Canadian hockey player father. You have to understand, we are in the adoptee land of the real/unreal. On one hand, I know this is my birthfather, and this sounds great. On the other, I have no idea what this means, what this really feels like if it's true.

I decide to follow this lead. I look in the Winnipeg phone book, maybe he moved back there after his hockey career. I found an Ezinicki, not William. I make the call.

"Hello," a man's voice says.

"Can I speak with Bill Ezinicki?" I ask.

"Oh, no—this is his brother John."

"Oh, I'm so sorry, I was looking for Bill. I'm an old friend from his hockey days in Pittsburgh and wanted to get in touch."

"Oh—he made a lot of friends in those days. Yeah, Bill lives in Boston now, he turned golf pro after hockey. He works at a country club now. He loves it."

"Oh, that's great," I say, "Where does he work?"

"He works at The International Golf Club in Bolton."

Yes!!!!! I can't believe he's spilling all this.

Then, a pause.

"Who did you say you were again?" he says.

"A good friend of Bill's—thanks so much."

I hang up the phone.

A quebrada is something broken

> A Quebrada is something broken. Literally, a break
> (from the verb quebrar). It implies the breaking up
> of the ground; a shattering of passes and horizons
> into a rougher country beyond. It can be used to
> refer to rugged canyons, a fissurelike ravine, broken
> and/or uneven ground, or the course of a stream.
> —Luis Alberto Urrea

(1988)

Something large had been broken in me all my life. I decided to meet my birthfather. I decided that the best way was to ambush him—I knew that he worked at The International Golf Club in Bolton, Massachusetts, outside of Boston. My instincts told me that if I called, he wouldn't be inviting me over.

Armed with two of my birthmother's pictures: one about an inch square with the right arm of her husband in a suit; the other a black and white from the fifties that she had given me: her in a fake cashmere sweater and a skirt, looking so young. I took off. My best friend Kathy said she would go with me, and we drove her white Ford Fiesta. We stopped about halfway in some chain hotel. I remember having a severe migraine that night. I was terrified. Kathy and I spread out tarot cards. I don't remember what they said.

I had called the golf club to make sure my birthfather was working the next day. The plan: to walk into the pro shop, ask for Bill Ezinicki. When he came out, I would ask him if I could talk with him for a minute outside. I was counting on the cultural stereotype that he would be willing to talk to a younger woman. The day we drove to Bolton, it was storming with sheets of rain. We pulled into the parking lot, and I wasn't sure that I could go in. It seemed impossible. What was I doing?

I ran through the rain to the pro shop.

"Is Bill Ezinicki here?" I asked.

"Yes, he is, can I say who's asking for him?" a man said.

"A friend," I said.

I wanted to run. Would he talk with me?

A few minutes later, he came into the shop. He was about five-foot-ten, a slim man—not a huge, hulking hockey player.

The pro shop man motioned to me, and Bill walked over.

"Can I help you?" he said.

He had a warm smile, a strong face, I liked him already.

"Yes, I was wondering if I could talk with you outside for a minute?" I asked.

"Sure," he said.

We walked into the parking lot. I led him about twenty yards from the store, still afraid that he might walk away.

He followed willingly, no hesitation. I liked that about him too.

I stopped, and by now he was looking at me in a very curious way.

"Do you know a woman named Dorothy Staiger?" I said.

"No, I don't think so," he said.

"Why, what is this about?" he said.

"Did you play for the Pittsburgh Hornets in 1951?"

"Yes," he said.

"Well," I said very carefully, "I think you might be my father."

He looked stunned. He kept eye contact with me, but it was like he was looking at me but not seeing anything. He was very calm.

"Why do you think this," he said.

This meant a lot to me, because he didn't say, "That's impossible," or "You're outta your mind," etc.

I pulled out the "young" photo of my birthmother and showed it to him.

"Do you remember her?" I said.

He looked at it for a while.

"No," he said, "I don't."

I must have looked disappointed. I was shocked that he didn't remember her.

"I was a professional hockey player," he said. "There were a lot of women."

"I know," I said.

"I'm sorry," he said. "Why do you think I'm the father?"

"She told me it was you. She said it was only one night," I said.

I was feeling crushed. I didn't realize until that moment that I thought he would remember everything. Now what?

He was very kind.

"Look," he said, "why don't we go somewhere and get a drink, some lunch?"

"Okay," I said.

He got his car, and I went with him to a nearby restaurant. My friend Kathy stayed in the car in the country club parking lot.

We sat in the bar part of the restaurant.

"What would you like?" he said.

"Just a beer would be good," I said.

He came back with two beers. Again, I am in the world of the unreal, sitting in a bar with my birthfather in Bolton, Massachusetts, having a beer.

I was really beyond happy to be there. It felt like an adventure, it felt energized, magnetic.

I studied his face. His eyes were green, sort of the color of mine. He had a great face—strong chin, direct look, a welcoming face. I felt that I looked like him in some way—his cheekbones, smile, but mostly his eyes. His eyes were mischievous, even then. He must have been about sixty years old at the time.

He was looking intently at me, also.

He said, "You could be my daughter. You look like one of my daughters, Julie. You remind me of her, you two could be sisters."

I was so happy that he said this, and that he wasn't trying to deny anything.

We didn't say a lot for a while. I know that he was shocked. I wanted to surprise him, in hopes that I would get a more authentic response. I didn't want him to have time to think about any of this ahead of time.

Then he said something wild:

"Well, life is life," he said.

"What?" I said.

He shrugged and said it again, "Life is life."

I loved that, and took it to mean that life is a wild trip, you never know what will happen, and also—that he was acknowledging that this could all be true.

We talked a bit. He asked about my life, where I lived, what I did. He wanted to know if I had a good life.

"Yes," I said.

Then, something strange.

He pulled out his wallet, stripped out a hundred dollar bill and said, "I want you to take this and get something for yourself."

"No," I said, handing it back to him. "I don't want your money—that's not why I'm here."

"I know, I know," he said, "but just take it."

"No," I said.

He leaned forward, gave me the hundred dollars, and said, "Buy some dinner for you and your friend, blow it all on one dinner."

I liked that idea, the idea of celebrating and blowing it all. I liked that he thought like that, the same way that I think.

"Okay," I said, "I'll blow it all tonight on dinner."

"Good," he said.

"I better get back to the shop," he said.

"Okay," I said, but I didn't want to leave. I knew that this would be it, the only time in my life that I would see him.

He drove me back to the parking lot. He was still shell-shocked. I thanked him for meeting with me.

"Of course," he said. "I'm just sorry that I don't remember."

I gave him my phone number. We hugged.

He walked back inside.

That night, my friend Kathy and I ate an amazing dinner in Provincetown, laughing and crying, eating and drinking.

I wish I would have kept the hundred dollars, to have something of his. I can't believe I didn't take a picture of him, or me with him. We barely had enough money to get home.

Life is life

"Life is life," he said. Two weeks after I met with Wild Bill, he called me at work.

As a graduate student, I was working as the poetry editor in the *Pennsylvania Review* office in the Cathedral of Learning, University of Pittsburgh.

My friend Deb, the managing editor, and I were reading manuscript submissions when the phone rang. I remember motioning to her, shaping my lips into "It's him!"

"Oh my God," she lip-synched back to me.

My heart thrashing, my breathing quick—I was elated to hear his voice.

"I can't believe you called," I said.

He cut to the chase: "I've been thinking about it, and I don't think I could be your father."

I felt a slam to my chest, the air leaving.

I had nothing to say, just shocked.

He repeated, "I just don't think that I'm your father."

I said, "But when we met, you said that I could easily be your daughter, that I looked like your daughter, Julie."

"I don't know what to tell you," he said. "I don't think we should be in touch anymore."

"Okay," I said. "Goodbye."

I felt the denial in my body/I knew he wanted out.
That was the last contact that I had with my birthfather.

Ghostdaddys

When I was a girl I was a boy with black boots and holster and a basketball hoop in the backyard. My reach was endless, I was birthed in a meteor shower and all the stars knew my name. Ever since, I've been on street corners with gimcrack men you wouldn't want to know, making myself a luminary. I had this piece of paper—took years to get it: the story before the story changed, before the government got their hands on it. I've been told_____.

My first father was a millionaire, his name on my birth certificate/voice on the phone/his lame-ass answer: *I didn't come inside her.* I was the small voice asking/he was the hammer coming down, shattering me into shooting stars. I covered my bedroom ceiling with planets, prayed for a meteor hit to bury the house. My second father was a hockey player who fucked my mother when she was twenty—I drove to Boston to meet him, armed with her picture, he didn't remember her: *I was a professional athlete*, he said, *there were a lot of women.* His green eyes burned familiar, and I thought he was a good man—then two weeks later, he said no, he didn't think he could be my father. I decided I've come from a long line of cowards, men who can only stand up if they're fucking/ flaccid after that.

Sometimes the earth moves in my dreams with lies about my past. I was bent on ruination: drugs for lunch and dinner—

with some dope in between. My face the face of no/father, unrecognizable/so why not? I was the immaculate cum-shot, I was the wildly surviving thing, racing after ghostdaddys in dreams:

Dear father, whoever you are, I hope the sex was ravenous, with cross/checking, slashing/I hope there were slats of light everywhere to see my star on the other side.

nine

the skinhouse

Like the dead-seeming cold rocks, I have
memories within that came out of the material
that went into me

—Zora Neale Hurston

Report from the skinhouse

I went looking for the body. The apple, tree, the river. Gliding voice, curve of arm, pearly blue uterus. Muscled calf, the neptune green eye, blood with the same taste as mine.

Why do I write my report this way? An adopted child needs to find a face.

What does a real mother's body look like? River, chalkline, bloody cave?

I am replica of nothing. *birthmother, conjurer, boneshaker, witch, let me smell your skin just once, I'll give you your bloody daughter.*

The bats resemble the deaf

> The bats resemble the deaf.
> But they are not deaf. They live by echoes, as we do.
> —Brigit Pegeen Kelly

Dear Birthmother,

You are:

severing the spine of memory. Moving and crashing the underground plates of the ground below my feet—before I know I have feet. The ground is not there. You are not there—a hole foreverafter.

You are:

PTSD with government papers. This violence to infants is legal—some fuckheads renaming it happy. You have "relinquished" your child. That's what they call it. Let's get real—you gave that sucker away.

You are:

a body I lived in. I heard your voice, felt your walk and the way you sat, slept, and one day expelled me. I resemble you, but I am not you. Echoes of all of that in me and today I'm walking the streets of Lawrenceville, your blood running through me.

Your very own,
American Bastard

A gallery, an enlarged passageway

> A gallery, an enlarged passageway within a cave
> system, links one cavern or chamber with another.
> Its ceiling is high enough and its floor broad enough
> to make it seem even more accommodating than
> other parts of the cave. It is a place where one can
> actually view one's surroundings.
>
> —Gretel Ehrlich

> If it is true that homelessness is an 'archetypal state
> of transiency,' adoptees have always been transients.
> They have a sense of being on the road even when
> they have a place to return to at night. They don't
> have the same relationship to things that other
> people have.
>
> —Betty Jean Lifton

As long as I remember, I was always running away. Hiding in the apple trees in the neighbor's backyard rather than going home for dinner; riding my bike past the boundary streets my adoptive mother named; playing "army" with the boys and wanting to disappear into another war; climbing into my attic hideout.

There was only one goal: to leave, get lost, become invisible. As a teenager, I would take buses out of town to other cities, then return by nightfall—never telling anyone where I was. My graduation present from high school—a suitcase. Samsonite blue, my ticket out.

But sex was the real escape. When my high school boyfriend was too shy or Catholic to go all the way—I found a married man for my first time. It wasn't great, but it gave me what I wanted—escape. I wanted to get lost in something, to forget who I was and where I was.

Drugs and alcohol worked even better. From the beginning, I drank for obliteration. Period. I saw no other purpose, and I started many evenings saying, "I want to forget my name." In the context of adoption, this makes sense—but back then, I just wanted another reality.

My MO— I changed friends, jobs, neighborhoods—just like an addict. I would wait until my lease was up, or my situation had deteriorated, and then give myself a week or two to find a place to live. This went on until I moved fourteen times one year, and then found myself with my mattress in the back seat of my '73 Chevy. Even then, I wasn't worried. Now I was hanging with drug dealers, criminals, and in danger of permanent obliteration.

Huérfano **is spanish for orphan**

> *Huérfano* is Spanish for orphan.
> In this case a perfect description of the landform—a
> solitary spire or hill left standing by erosion apart
> from kindred landscape features. Also called a
> "circumscribed eminence," a lost mountain or an
> island hill, it is a kind of existentialist monument,
> an island in the sky.
>
> —Luis Alberto Urrea

I was born an island in the sky—but I didn't know which sky? Why was I in the asylum? What were the rules here? An infant knows the separation—no mother and now a crib in a roomful of cribs.

What is at stake in the dream remembered? What is at stake for the dreamer?

I was learning, too young, about grief, loneliness, separation. The rules were: you were on your own until the strangers came. How does a child internalize this? Is this the birth of hypervigilance in the life of the adoptee: who are you and what are you doing to me? Is the infant starting to make distinctions between safe/not safe, what feels good/doesn't?

How to be a real girl

How to be a real girl—how to learn to "pass" was a primary torment of my childhood.

When I was with my adoptive family, I was always trying to figure out the combination.

If I did A + B, would that equal safety? If I acted like other "real" children, could I be mistaken for real? Truly, it was a life and death question for me, a disembodied puzzle of my daily life for as long as I can remember.

I knew I could never be one of them—the children born to "natural" families. But that was my motivation—to be "seen" as one of them, to "appear" real. But, how to do this?

As a young child, I studied everyone, looking for clues as to how to act, how to speak. My five young cousins had similar speech patterns, often speaking in a sort of monotone with halting rhythms. They were very precise and economical in their expressions, using some of the same language. For example, when telling you where to find a plate, they might say: *second shelf/left side.* They wouldn't say: *open the cupboard and look next to the cups, the plates are in there.* From them I learned to be measured in my responses—thinking that this was how "real" families acted.

I was obsessed with my cousins' physical similarities to each other. It was exciting and miraculous to see their long, dark eyelashes. Each one of them, the same beautiful eyelashes. I knew that this made them brother and sister forever. The way they moved their hands or didn't when they talked, the way they walked with a purpose. So much that they shared, so much to notice.

I longed for that sameness with someone—a body part that I could share, something that would bond us without speech.

In first grade, I was shocked by how much the other kids were talking. They seemed to be talking about nothing to me, and I couldn't understand why they were bothering. But, they were obviously "real," and I realized that I would have to start talking without anything to say. I didn't know how to do that, so I would start with questions like, "Where are you going?" or "What are we doing?" What I wanted most was to disappear, but then I wouldn't have a chance of being "real."

I started to imitate "real" people. In second grade, I went to Mass every day because of fear of death. Instead of recess—Mass. The blood. The killing, the blame for all the many sins, the black mark on your soul. If you died the day you committed a mortal sin (without confession) then—eternal suffering. It was the 1960s, and the Catholic iconography and teachings were devastating for me as an adoptee. In my young mind, I was already being punished by being given away by my birthmother. What would it take for me to be "good enough" to survive?

I was terrified. I sat in a pew on the left hand side of church, behind one of the regulars. I turned the page of the missalette when she did. I listened to her singing and tried to imitate the Latin words, which meant nothing to me. Meaning was irrelevant—I just had to do it right, or be condemned to death. That's really what I believed.

Meanwhile, the structure of oppression and brutality breathed freely in my Catholic school. Mrs. Reid, our third grade teacher, taped students' mouths, tied us to chairs. The boy with the brace on his leg was publicly humiliated when one of the nuns took his shoes and made him struggle down the hallway in the long line to the bathroom.

They were letting us know we were not "good enough," and they were. The punishments came quickly.

I felt trapped in this world of blood and punishment. Trapped at school, trapped at home. I knew no way out, and as an adoptee, I had to get it right or risk being sent back.

Dear adoptive parents

Dear adoptive parents,

Maybe you wanted a baby. To care for, love. Maybe you wanted it to come from your own body. Make a family, live that picture perfect life. Maybe you always wanted to be a mother and now your body is not cooperating. Or you want to help the world, find and love a baby who needs a home. Not overpopulate the world. Give of yourself. Service and sacrifice were always important to you. Maybe you traveled across the world to find this baby. Or maybe tried artificial insemination, freezing embryos, paying a surrogate so that it could still be "yours" (look like you). Maybe adopt an embryo—one of those magical "snowflake" babies. Or you're busy with your job and didn't want to ruin your body with pregnancy. Maybe you're adopting to save your marriage. I don't know you. Maybe you're a good person. You said it was the answer to your prayers. God had blessed you with a baby that you swear was *yours*. You said that. Even looks like your husband, partner, girlfriend. Miraculous how you can buy a thing like that. Maybe you wanted to give it back the next day. Started secretly hating how it reminded you of your body, empty. Everyone saying how lucky, how it's even better than having your own because you are saving this child. Everyone is lying. Maybe you love it, maybe you love it. Why didn't you go to therapy to deal with your loss? Not the informational adoption meetings, but the digging deep to see what the hell you are up to. To see that this baby is not yours, will never be yours, that you can't go out and buy a baby like a new car. What are you thinking? That you could tie it all up with a bow? You've erased a baby human to make yourself happy, to fill a hole, to do a good deed—at least own it: *it's for you.*

Maybe the kid will turn out, not become someone you can never love. You are stuck with it now. When you bought the baby, nothing was the same. At least the child is better off. A safe place to live. A past erased. No way back home. Maybe you're a good person. Maybe you're a good person. At least the child is better off. Maybe not.

Not that it was beautiful

> Not that it was beautiful,
> but that I found some order there.
>
> —Anne Sexton

My third meeting with my birthmother was in July, 1996. We met at a coffee shop east of Pittsburgh. By this time, my life had changed. I was teaching at the University of Pittsburgh, my first book had come out. I got sober and got married in the same year. Things had really changed.

This time, I was driven. I had to hear the "truth" from my birthmother, and I was burning with the need to know.

I could tell that she was different this time, less defensive. She said that her husband had died, and that she no longer had to hide her past. She looked great, with short blonde hair. It sounds crazy, but she wore capri pants and sandals, and an orangey-peach sweater. She looked happy.

She asked how I was.

I told her about my teaching and my book, and she was thrilled about it.

I asked her:

"I need to know who my father is."

She dropped her head down, and I said, "I really need to know. I can't wait anymore."

She was still hesitating a bit, her face starting to tighten. The flood of shame that filled her body last time was starting up again. She looked like she would cry.

"I went to see him," I said.

"Who?" she said.

"The hockey player."

Her face was shocked, she looked pale.

"You met him?" she said.

"Yeah, I went to Boston to meet him. He's a golf pro now."

She stared at me, sort of out-of-time. She didn't move.

"Was it him?" I said.

"Yes," she said.

Finally. Finally, that one word that I waited over forty years to hear from her.

I continued to push her. I just didn't care anymore about being careful or crossing a line.

"Look, if you were sleeping with more than one guy, I don't care. I really don't. Just tell me," I said.

"No, it's him," she said calmly.

"It was after the game, we went to Webster Hall Dorms where all the hockey players stayed. It was one night."

She looked up at me for response, and I was smiling, ecstatic to be finally in this story with her. It was like I was finally hearing something real from her.

She said, "I'm not proud of this, but I panicked and slept with my boyfriend and was going to say it was his. But later I got drunk and told him the truth."

I loved her for telling me all of this. She didn't have to. It was the right thing to do, but she didn't have to.

"What did he look like?" she said.
   "He looks great. He's incredibly hot," I said.
   "I know, why do you think I slept with him?" she said.

This was a great moment, where I felt a turning, like we had become two humans talking, two women—not mouths and bodies in this long struggle.

"Did he remember me?" she said.
   "No," I said.
   She looked sad, looked down at her lap, and said, "Of course he wouldn't. It was so long ago."

"I showed him your picture from back then," I said, "He looked at it for a while."

She had a sadness all over her face—her mouth falling, her eyes staring.

"He said, 'I was a professional hockey player. There were a lot of women.'"

"I know," she said, "I know."

"I liked that he didn't pretend to remember, that he was honest," I said.

She nodded.

"I really liked him. We went out for a beer and talked. I think I look like him a little," I said.

"Really?" she said. She moved closer to look at me and said, "Yeah, maybe the eyes and cheekbones."

"You think?" I said.

"Yeah, I can see it," she said.

I could tell that she was so far away, and she started talking about him:

"He was really something," she said, "he was the star of the team."

Smiling now, she said, "He was a good kisser."

This was great news for me. I felt like any information now was a gift from the universe.

Then she said, "You know, though—the whole thing was over pretty quickly. It wasn't that good."

"It wasn't?" I said.

"No, not really," she said.

"I wish you hadn't told me that," I said.

I didn't want to know that, I wanted to imagine the amazing moment of my conception as a world-shaking, passionate explosion. I was so high on knowing for sure who my father was that I didn't want any downside. She and I were laughing and talking now, though, in a way I'd never imagined.

Then, strangely, everything sort of shifted to the present tense. What do you say after you find out who your father was, how he kisses and fucks?

But very strangely, we entered some generic world of "family" that I wasn't ready for or didn't want to see. She brought some presents for me: some homemade banana bread and some holy water from her trip to Lourdes, France.

This totally freaked me out. I was so happy two minutes before when we were talking like women friends about life, sex, etc.— and now we are in the world of religion and baking. Like running into a brick wall, but a brick wall would at least be real. I know it was gracious of her, but it thrust me back into the world of pretense and how it's supposed to be, rather than our very real world of forty years of secrets and deception.

I thanked her for the gifts. I thanked her profusely for telling me the truth.

She gave me a permanent piece of life back. She put the bullet back into the barrel.

The fire roads, 2018

We're sitting in a coffee shop in Monroeville, PA—site of Ed
Ochester's amazing "asshole" poem, when I say,
   This is the place where I met my birthmother, the third time.
   In the wide dirt road of my heart, only used in case of a
bushfire, now ride the deep mud, the roots sticking up: I
know the table—back, left. She has on white capri pants, tan
sandals, a blazing orange top. She's on fire with what she
knows and I don't—the burning of my birth, and I push her:

You owe me this. I never asked you for anything.
   There's deadfall across the fire road, washouts and runoff.
Nothing's marked. She cries as my life opens in this stupid,
stupid coffee shop, and Don says,
   Oh my God—is she still alive?
   I don't know, I say.
   I'm trying to blast a singletrack, and rockfall litters the path.
   That's my family—I don't know if my mother is alive or dead.
   Don says,
   I'm your family.
   I know, I say, but feeling that pull into the great cosmic sea
and is she still here?

And now the running kids in the coffee shop—is it so hard to
know why I hate them?
   In all this maze of backburning? Their sharp, stabbing

voices and toy dinosaurs, but worse, worse—their fawning mothers and their baby talk:

C'mon sweetie, pick up your toys so we can meet Daddy, and my body flames up, fully involved, and I want to scream at this vacant mother:

Put the goddamn dinosaur down, this isn't your living room—there is no living room.

Is she dead? Don asks.

I'll look her up on the internet later, I say, *who the fuck knows?*

I look at Don, his eyes blue, blue, and blazing. How pitiful it all is—this burning that we're all walking, that we never talk about, really, because it would flame. It would destroy our small heads and smaller dreams, and so we speak in sweet searches for family trees and oh how lovely—while the fire road burns insides us, deadfall across a single track, torching us in our sleep—that fire.

ten

into the fault

Let's say I am in the hospital after a crack-up about
being alive.

—Michael Klein

People try to hide their pain. But they're wrong.
Pain is something to carry, like a radio.

—Jim Morrison

In toronto, all i can think of

In Toronto, all I can think of: I know he lived here. What streets did he walk down? My birthfather, Bill Ezinicki, played for the Toronto Maple Leafs as a hard-hitting right wing. Did he learn his brutality here, his post-season penalties for fighting? I walk to the Hockey Hall of Fame on Front Street. I see his name engraved on three Stanley Cup plaques: 1946–47, 1947–48, 1948–49. Unbelievable! Who do I tell? I'm filled with him now, imaging, dreaming, remembering. I'm tired of returning to the loneliness, but the blood tie is all I have—my flesh, how I got here—the story. Two guys come in the Stanley Cup room, I walk up to one of them and tell him: *That's my father! He won three Stanley Cups!*—and he takes my picture.

Four times across

Four times across. Before I knew my birthfather was Canadian, I was running all over Canada. I was *compelled* to go north.

I rode the VIA Rail across Canada four times. At first, for the adventure. The last three times, I was in search of: my past, my birthfather. Seeing the land by train, meeting Canadians on the way—was my version of a family reunion of sorts. Who were these people? What did they have to show me about life and how to live it?

On the first trip, the train struck a man on the tracks and killed him. I found myself talking about death with a man on board. We cried in the back of the train for the stranger.

On every journey, stories of bravery and survival: the exhilaration of the woman who left her husband of thirty years. A forty-year-old woman who talked about how she got pregnant and married at eighteen—and how it had ruined her life. People talk freely on the train—knowing they will never see you again. On this last trip, I met a great guy from Dallas who had just retired. He and his wife had planned this train ride from Toronto to Vancouver for years. She had died two months earlier.

These visitations bring ghosts on the train—the dead and

the living ride the crossings together: in dining car conversations, station layovers, and in the long nights of flashing lights and visions.

Visitation at Gogama

No shirt, was drying his long hair with a towel and staring at the train, he looked about thirty. I saw my birthfather young and alive, he stepped out of a brown house with a white sign on the side: WILD BILL (his nickname) in big block letters. I saw him the way he was before he made me—beautiful and astonishing in his maleness.

I tell you this is my family tree—no noble phrases, no grave-yards on the hill, just visitations. Now pieces of discarded track, explosion of purple wildflowers along the side, solid wall of rock five feet from the train, then a river/bridge/float-ing leaves that look like giant lily pads—is that possible?

We're approaching the town of Gogama, Ontario—small railroad town erased by the diesel engine. There's a bar called "Restaurant/Tavern" and a meat market called "Meat Market" and a motel called "Motel"—no other names.

In this place of no-naming or maybe first-naming, I decide I'll call myself "bastard"—it's plain and accurate, you can count on it. We approach a signal, a woman in a black tank top with killer arms slouches in a grey Buick Century at the crossing in a modified gangster lean. I decide I love her, call her free.

The choke point

> The choke point—the Achilles heel in a dynamic
> system where forces of flow and resistance
> bottleneck. For land travelers, the choke point may
> be a narrow defile where a path crosses a ridge at a
> point hemmed tightly by flanking cliffs.
> —Kim Stafford

Leaving Winnipeg, Manitoba 9:30 p.m. 8/4/14

The Red River, the park, all the stacked cars in the switching yard—TTX, Costco, SEACO, chain stores in the distance.
Fountain Tire, Peninsula Hotel, Pancake House. Three minutes and we're in the trees again, a half-moon in the sky, Scor-
pio & I can feel the deep secret of you in my body. A freight
train slams by—so close—double-decker cars. The energy
palpable through the sealed window.

I see the moon through the breaks in the boxcars—box-
car|moon|boxcar|moon| the haze around the moon tonight
over Yellowhead Highway. There's no stopping it: I miss you.
   Bloodfather, I'll see you beyond the moon. 10:00 p.m. now
outside of Winnipeg, the plains so empty in the night dark—
just the telephone poles and some stray trees in the blue.

Could I have been a light for you? Your blood still here in
me—crossing worlds—I don't know where you're buried, but
I know your heart is here in Winnipeg. A woman on the train

said it's the coldest place on earth in winter, but the people here have warmth—tough gritty town like Pittsburgh. Somehow you bring light to me now, even in this vast emptiness.

That's you. I feel like I can talk to you better now that you're gone. I don't know what that means, since you were always gone. Now—no way to meet you body to body—but your soul is here and I say hello, and thank you for the chance, for this life.

I keep taking these tracks West to find you—and now I have. You're here with me/on these plains, this flat, flat open. It's a beautiful space. The ground my new horizon line/the moon the only light as I roll into the new world.

You were in that wind

> You were in that wind, but you didn't cause it.
> While I stood there, as amazed as anything,
> this happened. And that's how I got this way.
> —Irene McKinney

The cracking/the splitting/the looking for a way out. From the beginning, the bastard child learns to dissociate.

I was the girl in the wardrobe mirror, the body on the floor of the city:

I had many ways to disappear:

I lived for a year with mattress in car, I left my body in my birthmother's crib:

I was jacked-against-the-physical/luminous with the drive of the almost hungry:
    Silver Warehouse of Dreams, are you there?

How do you know where you start and end if it's not against a body in the dark?

I come from the monolith, the everything that still needs burning.
    Great Cock of the Smokestack,

I claim the dark map of my renegade city:
  I'm still here, disappearing.

I am neither of both worlds

> I am neither of both worlds.
>> —Diane Glancy

There's a spreading wildfire in me that never stops, from not knowing my name for over half of my life. I found out that my Aunt Charlotte named me when the adoption came through. I don't have any more details than that—just that she named me.

She said she loved the name Janet—but it seems odd that my adoptive parents wouldn't name me? So, on my *amended* birth certificate it says: Janet Patrice Beatty. They kept *Patrice*, which was my original name. I'm not sure why they did that, if it was required to keep that name in some way?

In the continual fires of my not knowing, Aunt Charlotte was a great woman. She never married, was a professional woman in the thirties when women were barely allowed in the work force. I looked up to her, loved her. She had an otherworldliness about her—she went her own way, always.

She worked to support the whole family, and gave me a twenty-dollar bill whenever she saw me. Like some kind of sentry, she was a rock, a guardian for all of us.

She lived to be ninety-four years old, and when the time

came, it was the two of us in her hospital room. In those last few days, she drifted in and out of consciousness.

At one point, she said, out of nowhere: *I named you before you were born.* It was one of those moments of truth that just rises up. I was shocked. She didn't say: *I named you before you were adopted . . .*

I felt that somehow she had ushered me into the world—and now I was her witness for leaving it. It felt right to be there, that we had shared something between worlds in a way I would never understand.

A captured stream is regarded as "beheaded"

> A captured stream is regarded as "beheaded"
> when its headwaters are taken over by its captor
> stream, which at some point broke through
> the physical division between the two—The
> aggressor literally chops off the headwater and
> diverts the captured stream into its own flow, an
> act of stream piracy. Some misfit, or underfit,
> streams begin this way. Without the runoff
> from the headwaters, such a stream becomes
> too small to cut through its own valley.
> —Gretel Ehrlich

Wrong door, right day. I was falling apart, working as a waitress in downtown Pittsburgh. My Pontiac had broken down in Penn Hills, and I couldn't afford to fix it—so I left it on the street, with the SEX, DRUGS, & ROCK 'N ROLL bumper sticker intact.

Riding the bus home through Oakland, I was crying. Yes, crying on the bus. Pitiful. My best idea was to take a karate class. It would bring me confidence and help me to protect myself.

I got off the bus on Atwood Street, and went into the wrong door. I thought it was the karate studio, but I had walked into Pittsburgh Action Against Rape. At the top of the stairs, I turned to see a bulletin board of therapists' cards. I took down some numbers.

Straight home and I started calling. Some of the therapists sounded too traditional or formal, but with the others, I left messages.

One called back and said, "You don't sound too good."

"I'm not good," I said.

"Well, I can fit you in at 10:00 p.m. tonight if you can get here," she said.

"Okay," I said.

The territory between a bastard and an authority figure is tricky. With a history of adults buying us, stealing our identities, and then denying any problem—we have a few reservations about trust.

I went to the appointment that night and grilled the therapist. I wasn't friendly. I wasn't easy. I wanted to know what she thought she could do for me, what made her such an expert, etc. etc. I wanted to poke holes in whatever argument she presented. And most of all, I wanted to break her.

If I could get her to be "real" in this session, to express her own humanity in some way, then maybe she could be someone I could trust in the future. If she was giving me credentials and "therapy-speak"—or even worse, the dreaded, "How do you feel about this," then all bets were off.

Somehow, in this cosmic flow of events, I found a great therapist. She finally grew tired of my pushing and stone-walling when I said, "You're contradicting yourself. Earlier you said . . ."

She said, "Okay, okay—so I fucked up."
  "Yeah, you did," I said.

That was it. I knew I could work with her, since she was willing to own up to her mistake. Whatever force led me to her, I was grateful for it—I had found a piece of home. Even better, she was swearing in the first session.

You were the one who spun me

> You were the one who spun me into the fire
> of myself; I am the one you left behind,
> the one you saved while you were here.
>> —"My Father Teaches Me Light"

I think that everyone needs *one person*, one person who loves them or fights for them. A bastard needs that person to survive. It doesn't have to be a family full of cousins and Christmas and moral support. One person.

That person for me was my adoptive father, Robert T. Beatty. I was so lucky to have him for thirty-three years. He died in 1986. He was my lifeline, my salvation. The one person in the world who made sense to me. Salt-of-the-earth, he was a WWII veteran, a steelworker, the funniest guy in the world. He was kindhearted but a fighter.

He knew I was lost. He bought books for me when I was the weird kid who was hiding in the house; put up a basketball hoop in the backyard so that I could spend hours and hours shooting; bought a Louisville Slugger and a mitt for me so that I could slam balls into the house, day after day, breaking windows.

Later, he fought with me about politics, and when I wanted to move out west, he helped me pack boxes; he built shelves, fixed locks in my many apartments. We were both out of place in our separate worlds.

He taught me how to tell stories. He sat on the back porch at night with a longneck bottle of Duquesne, and I don't know what he thought about then. He made a rug for me by hand with the initial "J" on it. He said, "After I'm gone, you can put this by your bed. The first thing you feel when you get up will be soft."

My father, my heart.

An eater, or swallowhole, is a reach of stream

> An eater, or swallowhole, is a reach of stream or a
> tidal area given to violent currents and waves that
> often upset and/or suck under boats and kayaks
> and the like as they are attempting passage. When
> tremendous volumes of water flow over a ledge or
> plunge over the downstream edge of a boulder in
> the bed of a channel, eaters can drive boats down
> to the streambed before spitting them out again,
> farther downstream. The term swallowhole also
> refers to the place where streams disappear into
> rock faults, lava breaks, and tubes.
>
> —William Kittredge

The eater, my birthmother, was speaking:

I can't tell you his name.
You have to promise me you won't look for him.
He's not a nice man.

Agitated, frenetic, the eater falling into her own waters.
Sobbing, almost wailing.

She said:

I'm so ashamed.
I'm sorry.
It was one night.

I was swirling into the streambed,
lost in the downstream plunge.

I said:

> Can you just tell me his name?
> I won't look for him.

The eater filled with water, driving
toward the boulder's edge.

I rocked:

> into the lava break,
> into the fault.

10:45 p.m. and they're calling for third

10:45 p.m. and they're calling for third and final seating in Dining Car E, and I'm turning in on this night of half-moons and secrets—full of love for this life everywhere.

Trees now close to the train and I'm saying goodbye to Winnipeg, but never to you—bloodgiver, father, fighter and cross-checker—right-wing heart stealer.

The sky around the moon now white as clouds surround. A cloud crosses the surface now, in that way a face almost appears. No face, but beautiful just the same.

August 5th 6:16 a.m.
   I wave to a guy in a highloader. He's blowing his horn at the train, already working at 6:00 a.m.

The fields are electric green this morning—night after leaving you in Winnipeg. And the farmhouse redder, the red paintbrush? Burning the grasses of Saskatchewan?

There is no other way to say this, father—your death and return have made things gleam from the inside out—the dirt road leaping into morning.

The print, the signposts visible—your finger pointing the way through. The way through the past and now the endless saw-grass of Manitoba.

I wear the Manitoba flag charm around my neck in your honor/my blood. Now the blood is moving, the road found, the day of your blood completed. I am zooming into the present with you.

Asylum

This is the house I was born in. Look at it. Asylum. Narrate it:
Notice the sloping cornice, look at the curved windows, etc.
This is the house I was born in. The cast-iron balconies/ not
wide enough for bodies.

Look at the photos: three stories, eight front windows and a
wide door. Dark red brick/inlaid with brown stone. Women's
bodies/expelling/banishing/ Leaving the babies there. Look
at the photos, include the photos.

Containment

Containment. In this train compartment, the stainless steel breaks at an angle, hangs sharp. With the bunk down, there's enough room to turn around if you lift your leg strategically. Yet, I love this containment. Being *inside* of something. A pod. Not wide enough to stretch both arms out—ten feet long. Two-by-four mirror, three-by-four window, narrow storage shelf near the ceiling. Packed in like a dog, a fish—safe. I'm back in some womb? Back in the attic with the hatch closed after me. Containment as escape?

Bolt on the door—no way on or off the train all day as we wind through Canada. Why does this imprisonment feel like freedom and vice versa? I take pictures of the light switch, a silver toggle; slide the weight-bearing lever to lower the bunk/repeat: the scraping metal, the clamp and safety latch at the foot. The design flawless and comforting.

Freedom. The train runs ten hours late, nothing works. Knowing no one. Give me this room, a place—some books and my lover. I'm tired of arranging, talking—all the useless choices. I'll see you next lifetime.

The train stopped for the last twenty minutes/we are here. More here than usual. I love to be stopped, to be in that moment of nowhere/on the way to/but not going now/—what is that?

Waiting in the midst of motion, the million small minutes of it that will never be remembered—but experienced fully with the body. Stored, where? WiFi not working. Phone not working—we are actually full-body. Breathing, feeling *here*.

eleven

imagine a body

Blood is life. It behaves like a living creature.
—Patricia Cornwell

Say hello to my mother and father . . . the Earth
and Space.
—Jimi Hendrix

The term mainland suggests some immense solidity

> The term mainland suggests some immense solidity,
> as opposed to the fragmentation of land into islands.
> An island is limited and has a periphery, but the
> mainland is thought of as an indefinite mass, which
> goes on to the horizon.
>
> —Susan Brind Morrow

My birthmother lives in the center of me, and she lives outside of me. She covers all ground and yet I don't know her.
She is further than the horizon—no end to her. She gets her
power from blood—nothing else.

When I call her to arrange a meeting, my whole body shakes.
I force myself to use the phone, and my stomach spins sick.
Immediately.

"Hello," she says.
   "Can I speak with Dorothy?" I ask.
   "This is Dorothy. Who is this?" she says.
   "This is Jan Beatty," I say.
   "Who is Jan Beatty?" she says.

She actually says this. I'm her biological daughter. I've met
with her three times. Her name is on my birth certificate. She
lived in Roselia Asylum and Maternity Hospital, where she
gave birth to me.

"I'm your daughter," I say.

"Oh my God, oh my God," she says, "give me a minute."

A bastard often causes this kind of response—total denial or shock. The bastard is the dirty secret, the thing better left forgotten/never happened/purged.

"How are you?" she says.

Oh, just peachy, I think, but say: "I'm doing well."

"Are you still waitressing?" she asks.

"No, I haven't waitressed for many years," I say, thinking: *Really? That was twenty years ago.*

I say, "I was hoping we could meet this week."

"Meet?" she says.

This is the common speech pattern when a bastard talks to birthparents—it's like they are struck dumb. I want to say, *Hey, you're still involved in this—wake up!*

"Are you free on Friday?" I say.

I want to say something real, like, *I was calling to see if you were still alive.*

It's a strange feeling not to know if your birthmother is alive or dead, a moving ground that can't be stabilized.

"Oh no," she says, "My family's coming in for the holiday weekend."

"Oh," I say, "I forgot it was Labor Day, what about next week?"

She has no awareness that she's talking about her "family" as if the word has nothing to do with me—her firstborn.

The letter from the orphans' court

The letter from the Orphan's Court, dated December 21, 1953 and signed by John Freemont Cox, Judge—something that I find after my adoptive mother's death in January, 2000. Isn't that something I could have seen earlier? I am almost fifty years old before I read it or know of its existence. The letter is yellowed, brown with age at the edges.

The date of the letter makes me think that I lived at Roselia Asylum for the first year of my life, since the adoption wasn't final until then. The language breathes the propaganda of adoption:

> It makes me very happy to know that I have played a small part in a process which has ended in your being the complete parents of Janet, and in Janet's becoming a member of a family which is giving her love, affection and protection in the fullest sense of the word.

The *complete* parents? What does that mean? I have birthparents, blood-of-my-blood parents. Aren't they more *complete*? And how does John Fremont Cox know that this new "family" will give "Janet" love, affection and protection? Who's going to protect me from all the lies of adoption? There is no sign of my birth name in this letter. Where did it go? Who will protect me from my adoptive mother and her cruelty, manipulation, her wishing I was someone else?

"I know that you will consider her the finest Christmas gift you have ever received." It's good to know that I trumped the doll, the bike, the board games. I didn't know that I was a gift on the birthday of baby Jesus. The judge continues:

> The decree is in a sealed envelope because it gives Janet's name before and after Adoption and, in the event that you do not care to know what her name was, you need not open it.

This part blows my mind—*in the event that you do not care to know what her name was* . . . At that moment, my real name vanishes into the land of "was." Erased, invisible, it seemingly holds no importance. The new "parents" don't even have to look at it. The machinery of erasure (of the bastard) and protection (for the parents and the system) grinds ahead.

Finally:

> It will be necessary for you to consult your attorney, Mr. William E. Boggs, in order that he may secure a proper Birth Certificate for you.

This letter, full of men's names (including Mr. and Mrs. Robert T. Beatty)—is anything but proper. My adoptive mother's name has also been stamped out here, which was customary at that time for married women. Why was she so eager to lose her name? Did she see herself as property like me? Was it easier for her to erase my name since she never safeguarded hers?

The Orphans' Court is delivering property, and with great enthusiasm. The tone of the letter suggests a wrong being righted—rather than a new wrong being created. The bastard is born. Not in the giving away of the infant by the birthmother, but in the eradication of the child's existence in terms of name and history. She does not exist anymore.

ORPHANS' COURT OF ALLEGHENY COUNTY

JUDGES' CHAMBERS

PITTSBURGH 19, PA.

HUGH C. BOYLE
PRESIDENT JUDGE
JOHN FREMONT COX
WILLIAM S. RAHAUSER
JUDGES

December 21, 1953

Mr. and Mrs. Robert T. Beatty
1206 Kelton Avenue
Pittsburgh 16, Penna.

Dear Mr. and Mrs. Beatty:

        I am enclosing herewith a certified copy of
the Decree of Adoption of Janet Patrice Beatty. It makes
me very happy to know that I have played a small part in
a process which has ended in your being the complete
parents of Janet, and in Janet's becoming a member of a
family which is giving her love, affection and protection
in the fullest sense of the word. I know that you will
consider her the finest Christmas Gift you have ever
received. I hope that, in the years to come, the fine
relationship which now exists between you and Janet will
increase in its significance.

        The Decree is in a sealed envelope because
it gives Janet's name before and after Adoption and, in the
event that you do not care to know what her name was, you
need not open it. It will be necessary for you to consult
your attorney, Mr. William E. Boggs, in order that he may
secure a proper Birth Certificate for you.

                Sincerely,

                John Fremont Cox

JFC:vls
Enc.

609-1953

609-1953. That is my number. The adoption decree states that I am to become someone else this day, signed by Bernard H. Goodwin, Clerk of Orphans' Court and Louise McQuade, Assistant Clerk. The attorney handling the case was William E. Boggs, Esq. The document decrees:

> No. 609-1953, PATRICE STAIGER, BORN NOVEMBER 27, 1952, at PITTSBURGH, ALLEGHENY COUNTY, PENNA. to be the adopted child of ROBERT T. BEATTY and MILDRED BEATTY, his wife, and that SHE assume the name of JANET PATRICE BEATTY.

And there it is. A name, a number, a new name. I don't know how or why my original name, "Patrice," becomes part of my adopted name. Maybe someone likes it—maybe they feel bad for stealing my identity. Not bad enough.

No. 609-1953 Term, 19

IN RE ADOPTION

of

PATRICE STAIGER

WILLIAM E. BOGGS, ESQ.
1205 PEOPLES BANK BLDG.
PITTSBSRGH, 22, PA.

FORM NO. C.

Commonwealth of Pennsylvania ⎱
Allegheny County ⎰ ss:

I, BERNARD H. GOODWIN, Clerk of the Orphans' Court in and for the County aforesaid, Do Hereby Certify that at Pittsburgh, on the 21st. day of DECEMBER A.D. 19 53, the Orphans' Court of the County of Allegheny, State of Pennsylvania, at No. 609-1953 19 , decreed PATRICE STAIGER,

BORN NOVEMBER 27, 1952, at PITTSBURGH, ALLEGHENY COUNTY, PENNA. to be the adopted child of ROBERT T. BEATTY and MILDRED BEATTY, his wife, and that SHE assume the name of JANEE PATRICE BEATTY.

In Witness Whereof the seal of said Court is hereto affixed this 22nd, day of DECEMBER , A.D. 19 53.

Bernard H. Goodwin
Clerk of Orphans' Court

Louise McDanté
Assistant Clerk

Lake is a red pigment

> Lake is a red pigment composed of a coloring agent
> combined, usually by precipitation, with metallic
> oxide or earth to create striking hues such as
> madder lake (a fierce yellow).
> —Patricia Hampl

I am a bastard. I walk around in this body of mine.

After a year in the Asylum, I knew: inside the body of my
birthmother you find: a letter

folded/a globe/a life turned away from/parts of my body/
three different names and towns.

I am earth and metal/the slagheap and the ore/my blood
fierce yellow—the madder lake.

Sometimes I slide away. Sometimes I disappear.

I am truth, I am evidence. Go West in memory of me.

My blood is the blood of work and making, I can leave the
body and become land. I can make it all visible: See it all: the
red lake, how colorful I am.

Cremation

Cremation: that's what the website says. I'm in Boston, 2013, looking for his body.

As soon as I hit the city, I feel him. In the hotel room at the Associated Writing Programs Conference with my friend Allison, I say,

"I'd like to get in touch with my birthfather if I can."

I know he lived in Bolton, Massachusetts, but had only seen him once, 1988.

Allison looks him up on her phone, looks up at me:

"Jan, it says here that he's dead."

"What?" I say.

"Look," she says, "it says he died last year, 2012. Here's the obituary."

Something drops inside my body. I feel immediately sick, strange. Whatever feeling this is, I haven't had it before. But my body *changed*.

I have a hole in my stomach. I want to hold myself, double over—bury my head in a man's chest, any shelter. Roll up in a ball, fold in two/stay that way. I bend over in my chair/trapped. I can't breathe.

Allison reads the obituary out loud:

> BILL EZINICKI Bolton, MA, USA-3 Time NHL
> Stanley Cup Champion, PGA Tour Champion, de-
> voted husband, father and friend, Bill Ezinicki, 88,
> died Thursday, October 11, 2012, at Addison-Gil-
> bert Hospital in Gloucester, MA, after a brief illness.
> He is . . .

"Please, stop reading that," I say.

I feel dizzy, disconnected from myself. I'm afraid, I need to calm down.

"I just need to sit for a minute," I say.

In my body, his absence—but he was already an absence. What is he now? A bloodline to another world, to where?

I've been through deaths before. But how do I mourn my birthfather, who I didn't know, who is my blood? He was never in my life, so how does his leaving matter? My body surprised me in its response—*I felt him gone.*

After some water and quiet, I read the obituary:

> One of the most punishing body checkers to ever
> play the game, Wild Bill became the first-line
> right winger for the Toronto Maple Leafs' three
> consecutive Stanley Cup Championship teams from
> 1947–1949. He was elected to play in the NHL All-
> Star games of 1947 and 1948 and was later traded to
> the Boston Bruins, where he skated for two seasons
> before finishing his NHL career with the New York
> Rangers . . . unparalleled success from the game of
> golf . . . one of the greatest players in New England

> PGA history . . . accomplished career as a dual sport professional athlete . . . inductions as Honoured Member of the Manitoba Hockey Hall of Fame, Toronto Maple Leafs Hall of Fame, New England PGA Hall of Fame, Massachusetts Golf Association Hall of Fame . . . Player of the Year from the New England PGA three times.

I wish I had known him. I met him for an hour in a bar, and now I'm reading about his death, a year late. I think of 2011, how I was driven to write poems about him, obsessed with traveling to Winnipeg to see the streets where he grew up. I just wanted to "feel" him there, to see the sky he saw. Was he sick at that time? By the fall of 2012, I had turned in my fourth book of poems to the University of Pittsburgh Press, with many poems about him included. Did I know in my body that he was dying?

Now I'm searching for a gravesite—where can I visit him? Is he buried in Boston?

The obituary says:

> Private Funeral Services will be held under the direction of the Philbin-Comeau Funeral Home, 176 Water St., Clinton, MA. Memorial contributions may be made in memory of Bill Ezinicki to: Boston Bruins Foundation, 100 Legends Way, Boston, MA 02114.

Well, first of all, I'm really pissed off that contributions go to the Bruins. I always hated the Boston Bruins, and he won three Stanley Cups with the Toronto Maple Leafs—why not send the money to them?

I realize how ridiculous this is—I'm acting like I have a say, a ground to stand on. That's what it's like to be a bastard: you think you're part of something (blood), but then you realize that you don't even know these people. Your mother and father. A mind and body fuck at the same time.

I read further and see that his body was cremated. No body.
  No place to visit to *imagine* a body.

It's like a wide-open ghost town with dead air just hanging there.
  Where do I go to mourn?

I'm lost, I'm part of his remains—*don't try to bury me*, I think.
  What do you say to the already gone?

I am upright, alive—I am him walking around.
  If you see him, tell him I'm walking in his footsteps.

Allison says, "We'll go to the river tomorrow. We'll have a ceremony for him."
  "Okay," I say, "thanks."

Burial on the Esplanade

—Boston, 2013

I wore my belt of turquoise that Bobby made and the world
ring   I wore my adopted father's VFW "Past Post Adjutant"
pin of blue and gold

Allison and I took a cab to the Esplanade over the Arthur
Fiedler Footbridge at Beaver Place:

I wore the grey shirt   dark on front/light in back, the liquid
coral ring from the green ocean

I dug the dirt under the snowberry tree with a butter knife
from the room service tray, wrapped the jagged obsidian in a
poem I wrote. At the bottom:

> *RIP Wild Bill—*
> *I knew you and didn't know you.*
> *You are my bloodfather and*
> *I loved you*

I folded the paper over and stuffed it in the bear pouch with
rhodochrosite

Sun shining on the Charles, fifty-one degrees   1:30 p.m.,
March 9, 2013: parapets on the grey bridge

Pouch I carried for travel   for years   soft deerhide
with leather strings
   Wrapped the strings around 2X and tucked it under itself

Allison sang the offering song in her Lakota:
In a high-pitched voice but soft but deep:
             Here I have something
             I am standing to offer you
             Spirit over here
             here is something for you
eight times (in rounds of four)
She is facing the Charles River

I covered the hole with dirt   pressed down, turned in a circle:
   both hands up and down/both hands horizontal and out/
four directions, peace
   Canadian geese and mallards singing as we finish

A baby squirrel ran toward us   We stood in front of the
Café Esplanade

Allison with her dragon cane (with red nail polish to look
fierce) and broken foot with black walking boot in the snow
In the distance, the broken circle of the amphitheater

We walked to the side of a four-lane highway   flagged a
cab who amazingly stopped—
    Ten dollars, gave him a thirteen-dollar tip for the
carstopping   for the car that almost hit him
    on the four-lane by the Charles—for the offering

It should have been different, Allison said

I called the funeral home to see where his body was buried.
He was cremated, the family had possession of him

I decide I will get a tattoo on my left wrist on the underside:
| 12 | his hockey number

Written on the same hand as my adopted father's ring: onyx/
garnet; Written on the same hand as the paris engagement
ring: amethyst/peridot;

Written on the palm of my left hand at burial:
amphitheater   bear pouch   Canadian geese
Café Esplanade   adobe Arthur Feidler Footbridge
Beaver Place   mallard singing
parapets on grey bridge
baby squirrel
taking offering

All the men in my life present

I needed fox

> I needed fox   Badly I needed
> a vixen for the long time none had come near me
> I needed recognition from a
> triangulated face   burnt-yellow eyes
> fronting the long body the fierce and sacrificial tail
> —Adrienne Rich

No bodies present themselves to me. Mother, father, grandparents, siblings, cousins? I need a face, I need to look like someone.

When I finally meet my birthmother, she says that she had to give me away—there was no money and her father had died. At age twenty and pregnant with me, it was only her, her sister, and her mother.

My "maternal grandmother" is a woman named Mary O'Shea.

Dorothy (which is what I call my birthmother—I could never call her mother) tells me that her mother supported the family by cleaning houses for the rich. Dorothy's father worked as a truck driver. They live on Broad Street in Garfield, a tough neighborhood in the East End of Pittsburgh.

I have no photos of Mary O'Shea, but I make up pictures:

She's about five foot five, with a stocky build—thick in the middle with hefty arms from all the domestic work. She wears housedresses with a long white apron covering. I don't know what kind of shoes she wears—maybe those black old-lady shoes with thick heels and ties? But probably not to clean in. While Dorothy hides in the back room, ashamed and pregnant, Mary O'Shea leaves early in the morning to catch a bus. They don't own a car. Leaves early, comes home late. I think I would have liked her.

I find out later that Dorothy birthed five children after she married. Her husband never knew about me. So—that's five half-siblings from that side, and my birthfather also had five kids.

Ten half brothers and sisters who I don't know. Their kids? The word "family" lives differently in the mind of a bastard. Sort of like the word "home." Not happy words.

Dorothy tells me that she visited me at Roselia Asylum—I doubt that Mary O'Shea ever saw me. That makes us even.

She set me swimming

Mary O'Shea cleaned houses for the rich—she placed a fish in a body of water: her child, my birthmother, she set me swimming. My first house was a prison for children, orphanage of castoffs and secondhands. I floated on the surface of days, playing dead.

The spell of swimming can make an orphan dizzy—moving through the spin/to the plunge or the dip. You don't know a thing until you're in it, and maybe not even then. I found no furniture in the house I was born in—

there was no real house on Cliff and Manilla, just the hat-edge of the Hill, the brim of lonely. I was locked up, and maybe Mary O'Shea was locked up too—so, woozy, bewildered, I lived for the trick: the way to perform for the lifeguards of the body.

It would be thirty years before I knew my name, and reeling, casting my line for love, I picked nothingness as home. I worked in prisons, streets, and clinics—trying to free children from the bodies of men. Now I know something about what I did.

I'm still swimming for release, to say the thing that springs me free. If you want to do a good deed, tend to the monsters inside you—

As for me, you don't know a thing about me, walking around
  a stranger to yourself—

twelve

ocean of sky

I go outside and cross the fields to the highway.
I'm fourteen. I'm a wind from nowhere.
I can break your heart.

—Ai

You will be pulled from a womb into a city
—Lawrence Joseph

A floodway is a manmade channel

> A floodway is a manmade channel built as a branch
> or a neighboring bed to a river that tends to flood.
> Floodways are more common to Canada than the
> United States, and one striking example is a bypass
> of the Red River around Winnipeg.
>
> —Larry Woiwode

It's swelling on the Red River, and I'm looking for Wild Bill.

August, 2011, the Canadian pulls into Union Station, Winnipeg, Manitoba. Hours earlier, Stan, the VIA Rail Steward, said: *Welcome to Manitoba, where the state flower is the Prairie Crocus and the state bird is the mosquito.*

Now we see *flat* everywhere. On the approach, a parallel highway, power station, slag heap with moving bulldozer, half-mile train of dust left by a fifty-ton hauler, yellow wildflowers, wide factory lots of aluminum pipe.

First day, I walk down Portage Avenue to the MTS Centre—home of the Winnipeg Jets and the Manitoba Hall of Fame. Originally known as The True North Centre, and I'm thinking *yes, it's my true north*, my link to my past. Outer doors open, I look up to see photos of all the hockey players in the hall of fame. It's thrilling and otherworldly to see my birthfather, "Wild Bill" Ezinicki there.

A huge security guard walks up: "I'm sorry, but we're closed today. You'll have to leave."

"Oh no," I say, "I'm here from Pittsburgh. That's my father." I point to Wild Bill's photograph.

"That's your father?" he says.

Ed the security guard stands right next to me, he's about six foot five with massive arms.

He says, "Do you want me to take a picture of you next to him?"

"That would be so great," I say, and hand him my camera.

He can see my face redden with blood-flow, he can see me flooding with excitement.

I blurt out the story of the Pittsburgh Hornets, the one-night stand, the orphanage—and then something amazing happens.

He says, "No one's around. Would you like me to give you a tour of the place?"

For the next hour, we walk from room to room, with him revisiting the history of the sports center, the city, and especially the hockey legacy of Winnipeg. He walks me into the sports arena, startling in its empty white ice and absolute quiet. We are both out of time, in another reality, staring at the ice.

Past the high and lonesome club

Past the High and Lonesome Club on Main Street, Winnipeg, I'm walking and asking people if they know where I can find a vintage sports store. A guy directs me to River City Sports on St. James Place. Nothing there but new jerseys. I'm looking for a 1950s Toronto Maple Leafs jersey—something that Wild Bill might have owned or even worn.

I stop for lunch, and the waitress sends me to Kings Skate Snow & Surf in a neighborhood called Osborne. She says it's a long walk, but they have vintage.

I start walking, armed with a map. After twenty minutes, I find myself in a residential neighborhood, not sure which way is which. But I've got a bad feeling. It seems like an okay area, but I feel suddenly unsafe. I think: *I need a cab. How can I get a cab out here?* What happens next is inexplicable. I swear that a cab drives by within a few minutes and I flag it down.

"750 Pembina Highway," I say.

"Why all the way there? he asks.

I tell him, and he says, "Half hour in cab."

"Oh," I say, "how much? I need you to wait for me while I run in."

"Seventy-five dollars—more," he says.

He tells me he's from Punjab, India, as he texts.

He speaks in broken English: "You walking into gang shooting. People dead. You lucky."

"Oh my God," I say.

Three blocks later, about ten police cars and twenty evidence markers for shots fired litter the street. Yellow caution tape cordons off the area, and we take a detour.

I ask him, "Is this a shaky neighborhood?"

He laughs.

"Yeah," he says, "Somebody looking out for you, I never come this way. Yeah, I drop last guy around the corner."

He drives me to Kings Skate Snow & Surf, where the punk cashier with blue hair and nose piercing says, "Why do you want a 1950s jersey?"

I tell him about Wild Bill and he says, "Cool."

He takes me to a musty back corner of the store, where everything is covered in dusty plastic.

"Here you go," he says.

Meter running, I grab what looks like a fifties Maple Leaf jersey.

Punk boy says, "Man, I can't believe you found this."

"Me neither," I say, sending thanks up to the ocean of sky.

Later that night, I hear that one person died and others were stabbed in a gang fight.

He turned bodychecking

> He turned bodychecking into an art
> form, and he made sure his stick
> was on the ice when he delivered
> a rollicking hit.
> > —Mike Leonetti, *Maple Leafs Top 100*,
> > (talking of "Wild Bill" Ezinicki)

Growing up, I liked to hit things. A lot. I spent hours slamming the softball into the red bricks of our house, more than once breaking the small basement window. Whipping the basketball over and over to the hoop in the backyard was all I wanted to do.

For years, my adoptive parents grounded me for getting into fights with boys on the playground.

I was on the racquetball team, the volleyball team, the intramural tennis team—I was the designated hitter on the softball team. In college, I majored in Physical Education, but didn't last long. I only wanted to hit, to play—wasn't at all interested in how to teach it.

Playing racquetball with a guy I knew, I slammed the first serve into the corner—and he turned to look at me like I was an alien.

"You don't have to kill it," he said.

"Oh yes I do," I said, "Shut up and play."

I was relentless, brutal—more competitive than anyone I knew. I became someone else on the court. I had to win, that was it.

When I found out that my birthfather was a professional hockey player, it all made sense. It felt like a piece of my body dropping into place, a relief. It felt right. But when I found out that he won three Stanley Cups with the Toronto Maple Leafs, scored three goals in nine playoff games in 1948, led the NHL in penalty minutes two times, recorded 135 points in 271 games as a Leaf—I was proud—and I was home.

As I write this, October 11, 2014—the second anniversary of Wild Bill's death, I think of his fire, his brutality—and I thank him for it.

Crosschecking

My Canadian father fought the rich man's hockey wars, was known for crosschecking, delivering a bloody body block. He had an insurance policy that paid: five bucks for every suture needed to close a cut, and he collected.

My inheritance? I'm the designated hitter, the base runner, the racquetball king with the killer serve.

When my league coach asked me to demonstrate good base running, I hit and ran, steamrolled him at second trying to tag me. We ended up both in the dirt, me over him on all fours, his glasses broken. He got up, piecing them together, brushing dust out of his hair. Stared at me and walked off the field.

My father still inside me now, I'm free of the quiet asking. All the years of not knowing who I was has made me blood-hungry. He can collect his money, but he can never close the cut of me.

Switching

She's the designated hitter, switched at birth: she put christ's nails in her hands, she dropped the baby. When there was no birthfather, she bought shoes with steel toes and a big belt buckle. She saved the baby and became christ our savior, she bought the gun.

She wore it like a man/wore it like a woman, she said *suck my dick* and she sucked dick. She held herself close/tangled in her own wires and switches:

father of sky, dreams, and night, she was a slave to it until she called herself free, became her own man. In the steel wheels of her leaving, she became her own father.

An atlas on the underside

> An atlas
> on the underside of my dream
> —Jennifer Elise Foerster

In crossing the red lake to my old life, I find the world underneath. The world speaking its shaky truth. On the cab ride from the San Francisco airport, it opens again. The driver a guy named Thom from Southeast Asia, asks me,

"Are you in town for a convention?"

"No," I say, "I'm a poet, I'm here to do some readings."

His face changes, he gets that look in his eyes, that flash/then retreat that I'd seen so often.

"Are you a writer?" I ask.

"Oh, no, no," he says, "I work on English."

"You seem like a writer to me," I say.

He smiles, "I study. In my country, is hard to get education. I have done middle school."

He grabs three books from the passenger seat, lifts them up:

"This is what I do. I read these books. I talk to people, way to learn."

The cab fills with moving air as we roll down CA 101 N.

"Wow," I say, "That's great, it seems like a really good way to do it—can I see those books?"

His face opens, his brown eyes alive, and he passes them back to me. They are written in a language that I've never seen.

"This Burmese," he says, "my language. These books I read to learn."

"I've never seen books like these," I say.

"Yes," he says, "these are my books."

"Great," I say, as I hand them back to him.

We're driving by the San Francisco Bay, I feel opened to the air and the great expanse.

Thom hands me one of the books and says,

"Gift for you."

Surprised, I say, "Oh, my—" and look at the slim green book: the cover a waterfall with rose-colored flowers. The cover and inside written in Burmese.

"It is Buddhist book. I am Buddhist," he says.

"This is very kind of you," I say, and Thom nods.

"I don't think I should keep this," I say, "I don't know how to read it, and this is one of your books."

"Maybe one day you learn," he says, smiling.

I'm nodding, yes, he's right,

"Yes, you're right," I say, "I can learn like you're learning. Thank you, thanks so much."

Thom is very happy and saying,

"My gift to you," and I thank him again.

The bay still there, blue with its endless stories and upheavals.

I say, "When we get there, I want to give you one of my books."

Thom's face tightens, "No, no, not that. I give you *my* book. My gift."

I see that I've upset him and say, "I know, I appreciate your gift. But I want to give you one of my books too as a gift."

He looks at me in the rearview, his eyes serious, as if he's checking me for truth.

"Okay. Okay," he says.

"Thank you," I say.

I open the green book. It is all written in Burmese, with the exception of about ten numbered sentences in English. I open to the first English sentence:

> *1. You will be given a body.*

Biographical Note

Jan Beatty's sixth book, *The Body Wars* (2020), was published by the University of Pittsburgh Press. Books include *Jackknife: New and Collected Poems* (2018 Paterson Prize) named by Sandra Cisneros on *LitHub* as her favorite book of 2019. Awards include the Agnes Lynch Starrett Poetry Prize, Discovery/ The Nation Prize finalist, Pablo Neruda Prize for Poetry, $10,000 Artists Grant from the Pittsburgh Foundation, and a $15,000 Creative Achievement Award in Literature from the Heinz Foundation. She directs creative writing and the Madwomen in the Attic Workshops at Carlow University in Pittsburgh, Pennsylvania, and is Distinguished Writer in Residence in the MFA program.